MERLE ARMITAGE
DANCE MEMORANDA

Merle Armitage

DANCE

Memoranda

EDITED BY EDWIN CORLE

WOODBLOCK BY GORDON CRAIG

Essay Index Reprint Series

BOOKS FOR LIBRARIES PRESS
FREEPORT, NEW YORK

Copyright 1946 by Merle Armitage
Reprinted 1969 by arrangement

STANDARD BOOK NUMBER:
8369-0001-4

LIBRARY OF CONGRESS CATALOG CARD NUMBER:
78-76890

PRINTED IN THE UNITED STATES OF AMERICA

CONTENTS

To: George Beiswanger, Edwin Denby, Alfred Frankenstein, Edith J. R. Isaacs, Margaret Lloyd, John Martin, Stark Young, James Johnson Sweeney, Cecil Smith, Robert Sabin, and Walter Terry . . . whose perspicacity and courage have immensely stimulated dance interest in America.

FOREWORD BY CATHARINE BAMMAN

"Well—I seem to have made an impression!" In one sweep, my office door had been flung wide and with his "best foot foremost" (a forerunner of the later traditions of Grauman's Chinese pedal prints of personalities), Merle Armitage planted his foot squarely onto the freshly painted floor. That, back in 1915, was our introduction; it was the first thing I heard him say, and it was prophetic.

There must have been, I feel certain, a resound-ing note of inquiry in the lusty baby bawlings of the infant Merle, and I feel equally certain that it will persist to his final utterance. That keen seeking of impressions and tracking them to their source is in-nate. It guides and colors all he does; is in constant ebb and flow. Merle Armitage acquires impres-sions, he conveys impressions, and in nothing does this volatile ability reflect more than in his design-ing of books.

I

Since his youth Merle Armitage has been interested in art. His representative collection of etchings, wood-blocks, drawings and lithographs, which covered all schools and periods from Dürer to Picasso, once numbered three hundred and eighty works, but have now been presented to colleges and museums. He is the author of twenty-seven books, and co-author and designer of forty-two, eighteen of which have been on the subject of art or artists.

His dance experiences range from the period just before Isadora Duncan to Martha Graham. He has seen the ballet as both spectator and manager, studying the old as well as the new forms during the changing years.

He sees the dance as related to all things man does and is, and how it is indubitably linked with the other arts.

His passport to the dance, then, is not only as a critic who watches the parade go by and records his opinions and impressions, but as one who has known, talked with, observed in action, and savored the life of the creators and the performers. He has seen both sides of the orchestra pit.

In addition to his revealing comments, the book contains individual stories of Diaghileff, Pavlova, Nijinsky, Stravinsky, Duncan, St. Denis, Graham, and others, and innumerable pictures and drawings. It is a veritable wealth of material for the balletomane.

From even a fractional record, it is obvious that Merle Armitage has, in very divergent undertakings, registered importantly in the years intervening between the present and the symbolic footprint of "Young Lochinvar" there upon my office floor. To voice his own "prophetic soul," he has indeed made an impression. A woman's prerogative grants me the final word, and my own "prophetic soul" foresees that an increasingly expanding world will be impressed with his impressions.

DANCING GIRLS. WALL PAINTING AT THEBES

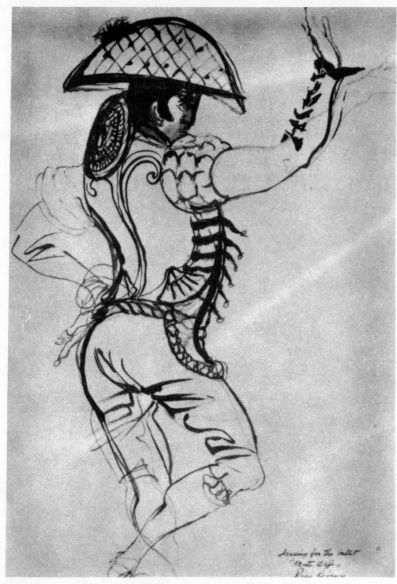

COSTUME DRAWING FOR MUTE WIFE, BY RICO LEBRUN

MERLE ARMITAGE
DANCE MEMORANDA

SATYR DANCING. GREEK, 400 B.C. (Walters Art Gallery)

THE DANCE 1

It was Gertrude Hoffman's somewhat vaudeville version of *Prince Igor* and I thought it was wonderful; it was also the first ballet I had seen, and I was a very young man. I sat in a half-hypnotized state as Borodin's music and the Russian aura swept me away to new worlds. Sometimes I think I never quite got over it. But I know better, because a short time later came another revelation — seeing the incredible Isadora Duncan dance. Even though sub-

sequent performances and personal contact somewhat tempered my earlier enthusiasm, the spell cast by Isadora remains, for me, a milestone. Then came Pavlova and Mordkin, who, stunning and exciting as they were, did not prepare me for the explosion which was to follow — the Diaghileff Ballet Russe.

I was familiar with the history of the Diaghileff organization in western Europe; and I had read most of the European critics on the subject of this organization, its stars and its repertoire. But one had actually to experience a Diaghileff performance to appreciate the power his ensemble evoked. There had never been anything like it, nor has any other entrepreneur provided such a sumptuous and lavish feast. A description of the Diaghileff resources will leave some present-day readers with the conviction that there must have been something vulgar, over-

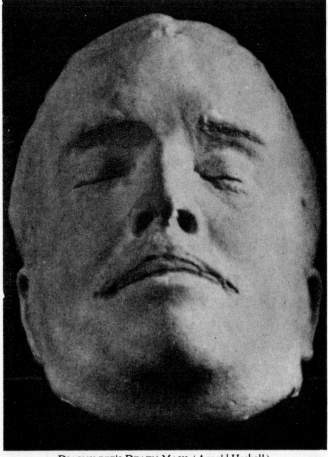

DIAGHILEFF'S DEATH MASK (Arnold Haskell)

accented and violently lush in such an accumulation of magnificent values. The answer is that many of the Diaghileff performances did come perilously near to such an abyss, but always they were saved. And the saving grace was the superbly disciplined execution and style. That style and that impeccable execution were the result of cooperation and collaboration such as has never before occurred in the artistic world.

When, before that era, have such aesthetic giants worked together for a common result, a shared success? From this standpoint alone, the Diaghileff organization remains unique. If, in the enthusiasm of the moment and in the legitimate intoxication of success, there was a tendency on the part of a designer of costumes or décor to push his undeniable gifts too far, always there was the restraining hand of Diaghileff. And this applied with equal force to composer, dancer, and choreographer. Back of Diaghileff was his cabinet, not a formally appointed or elected cabinet, but a group of men who had won his confidence, and who had demonstrated their right to voice opinions within this aesthetic principality. At different times Fokine, Nijinsky, Bakst, Massine, Lifar and other luminaries of the company were important in the councils of Diaghileff. But the small group which, from the beginning to the end, held Diaghileff's confidence and was objectively sound in its estimates, included Stravinsky, Gontcharova, Larionov, Benois and Bolm. From any angle, the Diaghileff Ballet must be considered one of the most extraordinary organizations to flash across the pages of dance history.

The groups stemming from Diaghileff, in fact almost everything which has taken place in the world of ballet since the passing of this curiously endowed man, have been an anti-climax. There have been other high points: the tour of the Adolph Bolm Ballet Intime, Roshanara and her company, that theatrical *hors d'oeuvre,* The Land of Joy, La Argentina, Lincoln Kirstein's Ballet Caravan, and the American Ballet, Escudero, Kreutzberg, the Joos Ballet, Teresina, Shan-Kar, Trudi Schoop, and Carmelita Maracci — all have been distinguished. But there has been only one Diaghileff.

A movement with a very different destination than that of the classic ballet is today bracketed under the heading of the modern dance. There are many practitioners and personalities in this contemporary manifestation, but the indigenous dance of our time has become sharply profiled and given its most compelling character by the art of Martha Graham. Hanya Holm, Trudi Schoop, Humphrey and Weidman, Tamiris, Esther Junger and Anna Sokolow have made definite contributions of importance; but Martha Graham, almost alone, has defined the terms and pushed the modern dance horizon forward.

The dance is as old as man. There are records of it in the Protolithic period of the Stone Age and it has always been a factor in tribal ceremonies from the Neolithic period to the Navajos. It reached great peaks in the Oriental civilization; it begins again with the classic periods of Greece and Rome; it reappears in the great outbursts of dance ecstasy of the middle ages; and it continues on through various movements in the 15th Century to that period extending approximately from 1650 to 1750, which might be called the Age of the Minuet. With equal generalization, we might call the next period, extending roughly to 1900, the Age of the Waltz. The Tango is a 20th Century development.

The three-hundred-year-old art of the ballet is, therefore, a great tapestry. Its various strands and patterns are woven and synthesized from all the materials of man's continuous preoccupation with movement in space.

For purposes of casual examination, we shall make an arbitrary division between the classic ballet and the modern dance. Isadora Duncan, although she did not live to see the flowering of the modern dance, made a rapier-like thrust at the principle which separates it from classic ballet. She believed that: "The whole tendency of this [ballet] training seems to be to separate the gymnastic movements of the body completely from the mind. The mind, on the contrary, can only suffer in aloofness from this rigorous muscular discipline. This is just the opposite from all the theories on which I founded my

ISADORA DUNCAN BY JOSE CLARA (Theatre Arts)

7

PUEBLO INDIAN CEREMONIAL

school, by which the body becomes transparent and is a medium for the mind and the spirit."

Isadora's uncompromising view might profitably be tempered by a less arbitrary attitude. The ballet has qualities which she may have overlooked or misunderstood. A great company, with well conceived choreography, and a masterful score, along with imaginative décor, all balanced on the fulcrum of an orchestra of symphonic proportions, can rise to superb heights.

Reduced to its final essence, the chasm which separates classical ballet and the modern dance might be thus identified: the ballet is founded upon, and is subservient to, tradition; modern dance is motivated by an original interpretation of life.

The ballet audience of today, like the enthusiasts for the modern dance, are primarily interested in the performance and not an academic discussion of it. It seems necessary, however, that a brief outline of the individuals and forces that have shaped these two forms is essential for an understanding of their aims and attitudes. The classic ballet, manifest in our day by several organizations including the Ballet Russe de Monte Carlo and the Ballet Theatre, stems directly from the Diaghileff Ballet Russe. Because of this, I should like to give sole credit to Diaghileff as the originator of this particular idiom; but that would be unjust to the man whom I believe is

most responsible for its contemporary character – Michael Fokine.

Diaghileff was a complex personality. His life and works are proof that he did not succumb to the decadence of the Russian milieu into which he was born. He was much more than a dilettante. He brought from Europe the first exhibition of modern art to be seen in Russia; and he encouraged painters, as well as an audience for painters, by founding an excellent Russian art magazine. But his remarkable qualities as an entrepreneur of daring and discrimination are best exemplified through his Ballets Russes. Here, he tilted against the gods. He was a purveyor of the extraordinary. He strung his pearls (his dancers, designers, choreographers, composers and conductors) on a shining omnipresent thread – the thread of style. Who before him had envisioned an organization whose resources included scenery by Larionov, Bakst, Roerich, Anisfeld, Gontcharova, Benois and Picasso; scores by Debussy, Borodin, Rimsky-Korsakov, Strauss, Schumann, Gluck, Satie, Ravel and Stravinsky; and a company which included Fokine, Bolm, Massine, Karsavina, Lopo-

ROCK PAINTING, LIBYAN DESERT

8

Two Dancers by Adolph Dehn (*Dial Magazine*)

kova, Vladimiroff, Spessiva and of course the amazing Nijinsky? His ability to synthesize such forces places him among the great organizers and directors of the history of fine arts. Fokine never could have created the Ballets Russes; but without Fokine, Diaghileff's vision might never have become reality.

Fokine was in a sense a revolutionary, but it must be remembered that he was first a product of tradition. He had studied with Johannsen (a veritable academic encyclopedia), with Karsavin, Volkov, and other masters, and was sound in theory. In practice, he was a seasoned performer of important roles in the ballets of Saint-Léon, Coralli, and the celebrated Petipa. He knew thoroughly the 19th Century repertoire. In addition, unlike most performers, Fokine was especially well-educated and had a philosophical, inquisitive mind. It was perfectly natural, therefore, that he should be disturbed by the state of the contemporary Russian ballet; that he would see its lack of consistency, unity and coherence; and that he would be impatient with its static, if not decadent, condition. If one finds the ballet of our time stilted and cluttered with clichés of movement and bromidic choreography, the Russian ballet previous to the advent of Fokine must have been a tiresome and tedious spectacle.

Lincoln Kirstein, in his admirable book on the dance, quotes the young Fokine of 1904, as saying: "Why was the style of a dance always inharmonious with that of the theme, its costume, and its period?" "Why," he asked, "in an Egyptian Ballet were the dancers in ballet costume and the supers in the dress of the period? Why did a certain dancer execute such and such difficult steps and what were they intended to express, for surely if dancing were not expressive it became acrobatic, mechanical and meaningless? Why was ballet technique limited to the movements of the lower limbs and a few conventional positions of the arms, when the whole body should be expressive to the last muscle?" To

9

COSTUME DRAWING BY BAKST

these and many other questions he received a stereotyped answer: "Because it is tradition."

Fokine knew that the entire human organism is the dancer's instrument, that conventionalized gesture should be employed only when it enhances or contributes to the style of the particular ballet, and that ensembles and groups as such could be used expressively and not merely as backgrounds for solo performers. But, particularly, Fokine understood and insisted that there must be complete unity, that dancing, music and décor must all aim at achieving wholeness of design. Nevertheless, it must be remembered that Fokine's conception of the dance was theatrical. He was a theatrical artist, a master of the *danse d'ecole.*

The joining forces of Fokine and Diaghileff was in a sense the converging of two great rivers. Fokine knew the weakness of the old ballet school tradition and already had plans for its rehabilitation along revolutionary, dynamic lines. Diaghileff understood the power of a new synthesis, and embraced Fokine's ideas in his grand scheme of uniting the great decorators, composers, dancers and choreographers in one organization, a great aesthetic laboratory from which were to emerge performances just as revolutionary to the Russians as they were sensational and stunning to the Parisians.

The meeting of rivers simile applies throughout Diaghileff's career. Such great streams of ideas and contributions as those of Benois, Stravinsky, Bakst, Pavlova, Nijinsky, Gontcharova, Bolm, Larionov, and Karsavina early became a part of the Diaghileff system, just as later it was joined by Picasso, Massine, Derain, Satie, Balanchine, Lifar and others. But in the incubating days, Fokine supplied the important new concept of ballet so vital to Diaghileff's plans.

For all its allurements, its traditions, the classical ballet remains an artifice, a synthetic compound, dominantly reflecting another civilization than ours, a rich and glamorous mirror of modes past. That is its chief appeal to the popular audience and, ironically enough, the *raison d'être* of its present enormous success. It is the panacea *par excellence.*

Any true historian of the dance must, indeed, be an encyclopedist. The dance recedes back into time with the overtones of a mirage. But as it comes forward and assumes its various characters and facets, we can see how infinite are its aspects. Beginning with the *Ballet Comique* and the *Ballet de Cour,* the well-defined pattern of its development is open to the serious student in many ably written books. But the classic ballet as we know it has felt the impress of literally hundreds of lesser men and women and a few giants who have changed its course. Salvatore Vigano, a hundred years before Fokine, succeeded in putting many of his ballet reforms into actual practice and revitalized the art in his time. Fokine and Diaghileff gave the ballet its present day character, while Massine may be credited with carrying these forms to an inevitable conclusion, the symphonic ballet. Symphonic ballet is not a new or a revolutionary concept as it is based on former ballet technique. In the showman's sense, it raises the powers of the traditional ballet to the nth degree through great music, breathtaking choreography, and idealized subject matter. Massine, however, has no such reserve of artists, décor or ensemble as were created by Diaghileff and, as a choreographer and director, he is certainly not a Fokine.

The classic ballet has an even greater popular future in America. Its very decadence is understood by the mass mind as elegance; its traditional forms are viewed as style. There seems to be no short-cut in the development of either the individual or the mass. Russia, which has experienced such great political upheavals, has not given us an aesthetic revolution. The theatre-going audience of Russia today seems preoccupied with the equivalents of the operas of Verdi. But it should not be forgotten that twenty-five years ago or less, Pavlova was only able to balance the slim audiences encountered on tour in America with a few good weeks in three or four of the larger cities; while today the touring ballet companies are among our most prosperous theatrical road enterprises, often playing cities of less than 50,000 inhabitants with amazing success. From the balletomanes which these companies are creating will come youthful and discerning groups who will demand more than an imported aesthetic experience. Indeed, there is present a growing audience throughout the United States for the modern dance. We cannot, therefore, honestly reject the classic ballet. It is a highly diverting "three ring circus of the arts" and to remove it would create a vacuum in contemporary life. Those who would banish it would, if consistent, also remove the Rubens, the Rembrandts, and even the El Grecos from our mu-

GAITE PARISIENNE, THE CAN-CAN (Victor Jessen)

I I

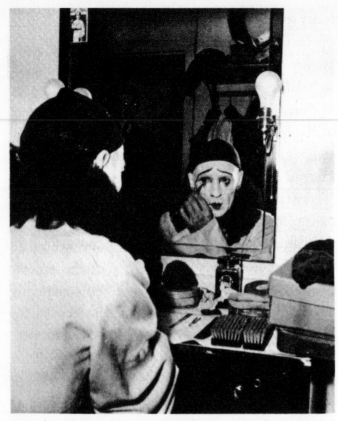

BOLM MAKES UP

seums, and the scores of Wagner, Gluck, Mendelssohn, Chopin and Tschaikowsky from our symphony repertoire.

No one can argue that this is not a time of transition. And periods of transition are both difficult and exciting. The academic reactionary fears and hates transition. It disturbs his dreams of the past. The alert contemporaries welcome change, for only through mutations can the world throw off its static, paralyzing habits and assume or adopt new forms. This is particularly true in the arts, and during the past fifty years, there have been more significant changes than in many century-long periods.

The first revitalizing influence in the art world was the advent of Cezanne. Painting had sunk to one of its lowest levels and had become the handmaiden of the most banal sentimentalities. On the wave set in motion by Cezanne came a whole battalion of men and women who saw the world with new eyes – the Juan Gris, Braques, Kandinskys,

Klees, Brancusis, Rouaults and Picassos who were representative of the vanguard elements in contemporary sculpture and painting. Parallel with this revolution in paint was a new stirring among the composers, a break not only with the tenets of Richard Wagner, but with the whole romantic schools of Schubert, Chopin and Mendelssohn. In architecture, great crevices appeared which separated the man who conceived of a building primarily as function, and those who were preoccupied with repetition of various periods of the past. It is interesting to note that these manifestations were concurrent with the industrial age.

There was one attitude shared by all of these seemingly disconnected forces. Each group had decided that it was time to overthrow outmoded and empty tradition.

Painting the surface of things was no longer necessary, profitable or exciting. That had been well taken care of through five hundred years of masterful draftsmanship. Music no longer need be either a soothing narcotic or a personalized sentiment. Architecture certainly should offer structures which would meet the conditions of climate, environment, and utility, and not a repetition of modes and manners suited to a more pedestrian or rococo society.

The physical world, having been completely explored, painted, sculptured, composed and examined – what paths, then, were open to the minds of men? For man certainly had become more, not less, interested in the problems of life.

In the world of the dance, one of the first breaks was indicated by a woman who came out of the west. Isadora Duncan, teeming with life, found the dance of her time without meaning. She was not the founder of the modern dance, but she pointed towards the road modern dance would travel, and all those dancers who have defied tradition, owe her a heavy debt.

DRAWING BY GONTCHAROVA (Russian Ballet in Western Europe)

Actually, there is no such thing as modern dance if one looks for a school in the academic sense. Like every pioneering endeavor, it has had false prophets and mistaken directions. Certain groups and individuals who did not realize the difference between subject and content, deluged the dance world with figures and choreography pivoted on the machine age. Others, painfully conscious of the simultaneous social upheaval, went in heavily for dances impregnated with "social consciousness," ignorant of the fact that the arts must make their contribution within their natural structure.

As for the audience, modern dance meant only confusion and anarchy to those accustomed to tradition. John Martin, in *America Dancing,* paints a neat and telling portrait of the reactionary: "Your first-rate academician is a walking encyclopedia of technical practices from the year one; he can tell you the number of hairs in Rembrandt's brushes, and can still be surprised by Haydn's *Surprise Symphony.* But of any genuine perceptive response to a work of art he is as incapable as his eyeglasses. In the dance he is naturally partial to the old ballet, because it has a code by which to work. He can separate each *enchainement* into its constituent steps, and compare the manner in which you execute them with the manner in which the book says they should be executed. The result is that you are either a good dancer or a bad. With other types of dance, he is less at ease. He watches closely for Renaissance hands, or Greek feet, or postures that stem from Botticelli or El Greco. Finding none, he must perforce pronounce the dance without style or technique. Face him with creative art which he can compare with nothing but the nature of man, and he is bewildered, angry and impotent. It is easy to see why modern dance has never been welcomed into this gentleman's bailiwick, and why our art galleries over which he officiates are generally known as museums..."

Although there have been many reforms in the dance throughout its history, the modern dance is the first real revolution. Heralded with a clarion call by Isadora Duncan, possibly its first practical

MACUILXOCHITL, AZTEC GOD OF THE DANCE

13

experiment was crystallized by Mary Wigman. Her contribution did not dissipate itself into the typical inflexible German system, largely due to the efforts in this country of Hanya Holm, an artist singularly sensitive to American qualities.

While Mary Wigman set in motion certain new theories, it was Martha Graham who really brought them to fulfillment. Martha Graham's arbitrary new dance statements were audacious to the point of sensationalism. And her audiences were sharply divided. Some sensed a new and welcome direction. Others were bored or amused. But the greater portion of those who witnessed Martha Graham's early performances were simply baffled. Bafflement seems to be the permanent state of a large proportion of the human race. Contemporary audiences were baffled by the young Mozart's "dissonance."

DRAWING BY PICASSO (1923 Programme, Ballet Russe)

DANCERS. DRAWING BY E. E. CUMMINGS

We were baffled and gaily contemptuous of two madmen named Wright who thought they could fly through the air. Friends of the man who invented the locomotive warned him that "if God had meant for man to be projected at the dizzy pace of twenty-five miles an hour, he would have built him that way." An audience in Liverpool in 1912 laughed and hissed at a first performance of Debussy's *L'Après-midi d'un Faune*. During the American tour of the Diaghileff ballet in 1916, a prominent citizen told me that such performances would serve only to encourage licentiousness among our youth! The world is rich in fools like Columbus, Newton, Pasteur, Lincoln, Edison — and Martha Graham.

But to maintain that Martha Graham is the only modern dance force would be as unjust as it is untrue, for some of the most significant developments have come through the collaboration of Doris Humphrey and Charles Weidman. Humphrey is a dancer of great sensitivity. She is without affectation. Weidman is likewise an artist, making his own patterns and creating his own direction.

Tamiris has emerged from a series of preoccupations with various forms of the dance, the theatre and the ballet, and has become one of the most significant of present day performers. Esther Junger has explored new principles of body control as she has steadily developed an artistic stature. Glück-Sandor and his wife, Felicia Sorel, in establishing the Dance Center, gave life to a most important project and both are fine artists.

The list of performers of the modern dance is impressive, including Sophia Delza, Warren Leonard, Elsa Findlay, and Anna Sokolow. A brilliant younger group includes Erick Hawkins, Sybil Shearer, Valerie Bettis, Merce Cunningham, Iris Mabry, Pearl Primus and several other highly promising dancers.

But what is modern dance? Certainly, it is not a system. If one were to state the principle of modern dance in one sentence, I can think of no better or telling phrase than to state that "the modern dance is a return to the nature of man." And man, since he dwelt in caves, has unconsciously used his body in a

From a Drawing by Van Deering Perrine

Isadora Duncan
DRESS REHEARSAL
METROPOLITAN OPERA HOUSE
NOVEMBER 21ST, 1916

COVER OF PROGRAM

functional manner. These movements hold within them the possibility of a language of communication, of which we as yet know but little. Only the slightest hints, verging on mysticism, are available. Why is it restful to contemplate a straight, unbroken line, the horizon at sea on a quiet day? Visually, the meeting place of horizontal and vertical lines, the cross, is the most static symbol, as movement in either direction is automatically arrested. And, of course, we have not touched the grammar of movement. As an example, why is there such exhilaration in the movement of recovery? Observe the downward rush and the miraculous recovery of a bird in flight.

The modern dance creator receives his strength and is motivated by the immutable laws of nature. He selects those forms which are naturally compatible, and constructs a new-old language of communication, design-movement realized in space.

DRAWING BY ROMNEY

15

DRAWING OF ISADORA BY WALKOWITZ

DUNCAN

2

Isadora Duncan was both a greater and a lesser figure than her friends and followers believed her to be. This daughter of a semi-Bohemian San Francisco family carried along with her a jackdaw nest of half-read, partially understood books, incredible affectations, plus an inflated concept of her own importance. This naturally attracted a following who could not possibly have understood or appreciated Isadora's underlying distinction.

Isadora was a meteor flashing across the world of the dance. Her advent was not only an awakening of dormant qualities in Europeans, Asiatics and Americans, but it was also the signal for a new approach to art. It is not chauvinism to assert that Isadora Duncan, an American girl, played a very decisive part in what was to become the Ballets Russes.

When Isadora Duncan announced her rebellion

against tradition in St. Petersburg as early as 1907, one of the men most impressed was Michael Fokine. She provided the necessary spur to his own struggle against the dead hand of tradition which had firmly grasped the ballet. Fokine never became a disciple of Isadora Duncan, but the new spirit which she proclaimed was the motivation in his reforms.

Diaghileff assigns to Duncan a most important place in his own early progression. It was she who demonstrated with such eloquence that great music must be re-created in dance movement, as against the traditional concept that one danced or performed to the music. On the personal side, Isadora was essentially an individual of uncommon sincerity with a mind and body dedicated to what she believed to be the greatest cause. There was iron in her will. However, there is little in her actions, her manners, her background or her avowed credo, which can account for the part she played or her singular accomplishments; for she actually changed the attitude of an entire generation and her spirit is still very much alive.

It in no way minimizes the extraordinary qualities of Isadora Duncan, either as artist or person, to be conscious that the influence which she exerted was enhanced by perfect timing. Consciously or unconsciously, Isadora Duncan rode on a wave of multiple forces, a natural, youthful reaction to the stuffiness and the banalities which characterized the Gay Nineties.

Proper timing has catapulted many persons into fame. Jascha Heifetz played his American debut at Carnegie Hall at a time when no great artist had appeared on the scene since the day, many years previous, when an audience feverishly acclaimed the blond and captivating Mischa Elman. Although several highly endowed violinists made their first American appearances within several weeks after the Heifetz debut, the youthful Russian already had captured the imagination of American concert goers and there was no place at the moment for other gods.

Isadora Duncan rode a larger, a more significant, wave of public approval. Whereas Heifetz by his impeccable technique won an audience of sophistication and considerable musical stature, Isadora Duncan personified a new freedom related to every element of our national life.

DRAWING BY LAFITTE

She represented an escape from the pretentious, ugly houses, cluttered with what-nots, lace curtains, gilded tennis racquets, and other rustic or grotesque bric-a-brac of the time. She represented release from steel-stayed corsets and a dozen petticoats. But more significant than these or other material things was the psychological impact of this beautiful young woman dancing barefoot in a Grecian tunic; a dance largely improvised through the immediate emotional sway of the music of Beethoven, Tschaikowsky or Chopin. Every young girl who saw these performances, and all the tens of thousands who read about them and the artist in newspapers and magazines, were impelled, at least mentally, to throw off the restraints of family admonitions and, figuratively, to run barefoot through the dewy grass in loosely flowing robes. Isadora Duncan, as symbol, represented youth's age-old desire for emancipation.

Unless the essential meaning of Isadora is understood, she verges perilously close to the bogus. Superficially she had many characteristics of the mountebank. Break Isadora down into her component affectations and eccentricities, and she was exasperatingly capricious and childishly willful. She embraced absurd social theories in her crusades for justice, truth and equality. In practice, she was wantonly wasteful of other people's feelings, time, and especially their money.

But she was imbued with the conviction, industry, and zeal which have characterized reformers from Martin Luther to Trotsky. She was the apostle of action, untrammeled by plans or meditation. She would change the world from stupidity to awareness, from evil to good, from ugliness to beauty, from prejudice to understanding, and she would change it immediately!

Isadora's star was well past its ascendency when I had my fleeting contacts with her. Those clearly remembered moments had to do with publicity, with programs, with the knotty problems posed by arbitrary cancellation of engagements.

Chaos is far too limited a word to describe either the locale or the atmosphere of those brief interviews. In hotel suites, piled high with trunks, clothes, costumes, and defunct breakfast trays — a disorder which seemed ingenious if not inspired — Isadora reigned, the center of a group of interviewers, couturières, managers, and just plain hangers-on. Appalled at the idea of receiving answers to my questions or making any progress whatever in such a milieu, I nevertheless remember that decisions were somehow made, that my flustered,

youthful appearance, but tenaciously insistent attitude, was neither ignored nor ridiculed. Indeed, in proper turn she gave me her undivided attention for as much as five minutes. At those times she loved me (she would, I hazard, have loved anyone momentarily) because I gave her homage, and endorsed her world and her important place in it.

What was the dance of Isadora Duncan?

To see her again in memory, I must look back through an impressive vista of great artists of the dance; past the compelling immediacy of Martha Graham, past the images evoked by Mary Wigman, the intoxication of Argentina, the poetry and romance of Anna Pavlova; past that merger of aes-

PORTRAIT OF ISADORA BY BAKST

18

thetic and muscular exhibition which was Nijinsky; back through lines of noble figures which include Carmelita, Roshanara, Mordkin, Bolm, Massine, Lifar, Karsavina, and a dozen others. And there – on bare boards, with a great orchestra between her and the audience – is Isadora. She prances across the stage, stops, lifts one hand to her ear to catch some whisper from the gods, and as an orchestral passage gains momentum to a crescendo, she creates before my eyes, unassisted by props or scenery, a world of pagan poetry which, somehow, still seems alive, fresh, and unique.

Yet, not discounting the spell of her most effective moments, I distinctly recall many measures where lack of discipline, uncertainty, and unrealized intention intervened. But the powerful and undeniable communication which penetrated well beyond the walls of halls and theatres, was there, and it eluded, as does all great art, semantic analysis.

I remember a party Max Eastman gave for Isadora Duncan. She sat on the floor discussing the dance with a group of friends. Max Eastman deplored the evanescence of the dancer's art, and pleaded to have a motion picture made for posterity of Isadora's particular contribution.

"No," protested Isadora. "I want no visual record whatever to remain of my dancing. I wish to become entirely a legend. After I am gone people will ask, 'How did Isadora dance?' And no one will be able to tell how Isadora danced!"

DIAGHILEFF

3

Even before the tidal wave of revolution swept over Russia, it was was extremely difficult to document the life of Sergei Pavlovitch Diaghileff. Many celebrated men have been prolific letter-writers; Diaghileff was not. Most men in public life have confided in someone close to them; few people received Diaghileff's confidence. He was not interested in personal publicity or aggrandizement, and he kept his own counsel to an uncommon degree.

From 1909 to 1929 Diaghileff dominated the artistic life of Europe, influencing its music, its painting, its sculpture, and certainly its fashions. It is interesting to speculate on what might have been the careers of Boris Anisfeld, Leon Bakst, Alexandre Benois, Adolph Bolm, Michael Fokine, Serge Grigorieff, Tamara Karsavina, Constantine Korovin, Serge Lifar, Lydia Lopokova, Leonide Massine, Vaslav Nijinsky, Walter Nouvel, Anna

Pavlova, Nicholas Roerich, Ida Rubinstein, and Igor Stravinsky without the galvanizing leadership of his peculiar genius.

Conversations with a dozen men who knew Diaghileff will produce twelve different versions of him. I saw him in action during his first American tour and have known several persons who knew him as intimately as anyone could know him. From these contacts and observations, plus research, the following general picture of his career has been constructed.

A man must be judged by his time, his environment, and his objectives. Sergei Diaghileff was born into a Russia not yet emerged from its centuries of serfdom. There were Tzar, Grand Dukes, nobility, a comparatively few wealthy merchants, and peasants. There was no middle class such as we know in this country. His immediate environment, important in shaping his future, was a group of young bloods who called themselves the "Pickwickians." They were sons of well-to-do parents enrolled in an exclusive private school.

The young Russian schoolboy was not, as in this country, largely concerned with sports and games. Nor were they long-haired bespectacled members of the so-called "intelligentsia." They were as gay and spirited as any other group of young men and quite as irresponsible, but their hobbies and enthusiasms were concerned with discussions of art, social theories, and the little known scientific world. Leon Bakst and Alexandre Benois were members of this group as was Walter Nouvel. In August 1890 young Sergei Diaghileff joined this group. Sergei was the son of an Army officer who had grown up in Perm, at that time the cultural center of the Ural province. Sergei was a handsome youth, plump, ruddy of complexion, with a sensuous mouth, and something of a fop.

Diaghileff early began to demonstrate a quality which was to take him far — an ability to organize,

backed by an indomitable will. Anyone familiar with Russians knows the fine quality of their imaginations and their endless projects, which usually remain just that. Diaghileff became, in this little group, the man of action. His first project was the organization of his group into what is known in Russian history as *Mir Iskustva* (The World of

PORTRAIT OF BAKST BY PICASSO

Art). It is difficult to state the purposes, the policies and the program of *Mir Iskustva*, but it did produce an art journal, it organized exhibitions and it gave character to the artistic life and spearheaded the Russian cultural exploits of its time. The magazine *Mir Iskustva* would have been an elegant art journal in any country; in the St. Petersburg of those days it was magnificent.

Mir Iskustva as a group embraced the most promising of Russia's young creative talent and it was not long until the Director of Imperial Theatres enlisted two of its members as junior assistants, one of them being Diaghileff. Flushed with success, Diaghileff insisted on producing a ballet, and immediately a delegation of the Imperial Theatres' directors protested against trusting a junior assistant with such an important commission. This led to a real collision of wills which resulted in the directors demanding Diaghileff's resignation. Dismissal was a much more serious event than was first realized, for it not only cut Diaghileff's contacts with the Imperial Theatres, but it was to hamper his whole subsequent career in Russia. Except for the patronage of Grand Duke Vladimir Alexandrovitch, Diaghileff apparently never succeeded in completely winning the Russian Court circles nor did he have their full support in his various enterprises.

He temporarily abandoned his theatre projects and brought to Russia its first exhibitions of European art. In 1905 he organized an exhibition of Russian portraits, devoting to it the same amazing energy which later was to make him a world figure. He traveled over a large portion of Russia visiting out of the way museums and estates to collect pictures. The result was the first important showing of Russian paintings ever exhibited.

Diaghileff's progressive activities inevitably earned the jealousy and the displeasure of many men in high places, including certain Grand Dukes who, in turn, prejudiced the Tzar. On the opening night Diaghileff accompanied the Tzar through the exhibition and differences of opinion became so obvious that he decided upon a move affecting his entire future career; he would take the exhibition to Paris.

Mir Iskustva hoped to act as a medium for the exchange of ideas between Russia and the West, and a Western crusade had never been its paramount objective. It would be a mistake also to explain Diaghileff's European plans entirely by his failure to obtain full support in Russia. It was

a case of necessity. Russian indifference had frustrated original plans and the group turned West as its only opportunity of continuing its artistic projects.

The exhibition of Russian portraits organized by Diaghileff was taken to Paris in 1906, occupying twelve halls of the *Salon de Automne*. Leon Bakst decorated the galleries, Diaghileff published a remarkable catalogue, and Alexandre Benois read a provocative paper on Russian art. Paris was fascinated.

Diaghileff undertook his second Parisian enterprise in 1907. This was a series of Russian concerts, bringing to France a brilliant company of performers, each of whom was to achieve world fame. Paris heard for the first time Feodor Chaliapin. The youthful Rachmaninoff played the piano. Rimsky-Korsakov, Alexandre Scriabin, and Josef Hofmann gave further distinction to this unique undertaking, and Arthur Nikisch, at the moment a Russian idol, conducted. Undoubtedly, it was the most brilliant performance of Russian music ever to be heard in Paris.

Diaghileff was beginning to build a solid reputation in France, and in 1908 he added further laurels with his first theatrical venture, a production of Moussorgsky's *Boris Godounov* with the transcendent Chaliapin in the title role. The success of this performance was striking. It was repeated eight times at the Paris Opera.

In the meantime, Benois had become interested in the idea of producing a ballet on the subject of *Le Pavillon d'Armide* for which Tcherepnin composed the score. This was offered at the time to the Director of the Imperial Theatres, but no agreement was reached. In 1907 there seemed to be an opportunity to present *Le Pavillon d'Armide* in Paris at the Opera Comique. Benois spent an entire summer in St. Petersburg working on scenery and costumes and it was during this period that he first met

Michael Fokine. Even as a young man, Fokine was considered a first-rate dancer and an original choreographer, and Benois was certainly in need of such resources. Fokine was immediately commissioned to create the choreography for *Le Pavillon d'Armide*. Fokine, in turn, introduced Benois to a very promising young dancer whose name was Nijinsky.

A first performance of *Le Pavillon d'Armide* was arranged to take place in the Imperial Theatres in St. Petersburg. Benois invited Diaghileff to a rehearsal, but as he was about to enter the theatre a police inspector ordered him to leave. Diaghileff's every contact with officialdom seemed doomed to failure.

When the Imperial Theatres commanded that Benois give a first performance of his ballet without the advantage of a dress rehearsal, Benois considered himself the victim of a plot to ruin his production, and gave an interview to the press denouncing all the directors of the Imperial Theatres. This had a surprising result, for the head Director, reversing himself, ordered a performance with *two* dress rehearsals. More difficulties followed. The leading ballerina, obviously annoyed because of the second rehearsal, refused to dance the role of Armide and Benois' position was desperate. The afternoon before the final dress rehearsal, Benois encountered Anna Pavlova, a young dancer, and confided his predicament. Pavlova decided to risk her own reputation and danced the role, achieved a great success, and won the lasting friendship of Benois. Diaghileff, through friends at court, managed to attend the performance. Enthusiastic, he immediately decided that *Le Pavillon d'Armide* must be presented in Paris.

Following the great success of his *Boris Godounov,* Diaghileff planned to return to Paris with a season of combined opera and ballet. Bakst had discovered a strikingly beautiful girl with a great talent, Ida Rubinstein, and it was decided to give her the leading role in the ballet *Cleopâtre.* Diaghileff augmented his program of ballet and opera with two more ballets, including the now celebrated *Les Sylphides,* and *Prince Igor* to his opera repertoire.

COVER OF MIR ISKUSTVA

This memorable season was the true inception of "Les Ballets Russes de Serge de Diaghilew." Although Paris applauded Russian opera, these productions had no such exotic flavor as the ballets which far overshadowed all other performances. The *Mir Iskustva* group, headed by Diaghileff, had found its true vocation. The die was cast. They had run the gantlet from art magazines to exhibitions of painting; from concert music to opera. Finally, they realized their future must be concerned with ballet and nothing else. Ballet was the international language, and as produced by the group it presented the greatest opportunity for creative imagination and gave the fullest scope to the resources of this particularly prolific organization.

The world knows the rest of the story. Europe was to experience a Diaghileff Ballet Russe fever, every European capital was to have its seasonal visit by this organization. Stravinsky was to electrify the most sophisticated audiences with his *Petrouchka, L'Oiseau de Feu* and later his monumental *Le Sacre du Printemps.* The careers of Karsavina, Bolm, Massine and other stars were to mature, and Nijinsky was to become the most sensational dancer of his time. Pavlova, after achieving signal success and a great name in Europe, was to depart and form her own company. Such men as Picasso, Matisse, Cocteau, Satie and Ravel were to join Diaghileff's forces. Every balletomane is familiar with this new fusing of the arts, and with the momentum given to the classic ballet by Diaghileff.

Few realize, however, that the ballets which made Diaghileff's fame were in no sense typically or traditionally Russian. The Imperial Ballet Schools were, in a sense, monastic. Theirs was an atmosphere of rigid discipline. Children entering the school parted company with their parents to begin a life of regimented study and physical exercise. The Maryinsky Theatre had the odor of a hot-house. Everything was subservient to tradition. The conventional style of ballet dominated. There was no conception of the ballet as a unity. A performance was divided into special numbers as old style Italian opera alternated between arias, duets and choruses. The *prima ballerina,* for instance, always came forward for her solo dance, the *corps de ballet* meanwhile remaining upstage. Everything including choreography was stilted, cut and dried.

Diaghileff came into this static scene with the dynamism of a tornado. His conception of the ballet was a synthesis of all the arts: décor by the greatest painters, music by the greatest composers, costumes by new and daring designers, choreog-

raphy which gave meaning to a ballet, great dancers with freedom to give a highly individualized performance, and a company imbued with the idea of *dancing* the music, not dancing *to* it. Diaghileff was profoundly aware that the ballet revolution must be made in what the Army terms "a company front," meaning that all values and elements must march together.

Diaghileff's first success in Paris was a prerequisite to the future of the Ballets Russes, which were as baffling and unconventional to the Russians of St. Petersburg and Moscow as they were stimulating and exciting to the Parisians. Diaghileff's enemies at home and his lack of encouragement from the Tzar, often placed his projects in jeopardy. Finances were often withheld on the most capricious basis, and more than once passports were refused the company about to depart for its scheduled European season. Many sincere Russians believed that Diaghileff was misrepresenting the Russian scene to the Western world. Only a man of tremendous convictions and extraordinary will could have survived the difficulties faced by Diaghileff at home and abroad.

World War I had brought a temporary end to Diaghileff's European seasons. In 1915 he took a villa near his friend, Igor Stravinsky, in Switzerland. The company was disbanded and the future looked dark, indeed. Then came Otto Kahn's offer of an American tour accompanied by a handsome cash advance, enabling Diaghileff to reassemble the company and hold a series of rehearsals in Switzerland.

I had always thought of Diaghileff as an enormous man, but actually he was of medium size. His neck overlapping with folds of flesh bulged over his collar; his head seemed too large for his body, he had a fine expanse of brow, his eyes were deep, penetrating and luminous, and he had a sensual, animal mouth. When I first saw him, it occurred to me that here was a Russian version of a more muscular and dominant Oscar Wilde. His arrival in America with his company both saved and revitalized Diaghileff and his ballet.

On tour, this fantastic entourage traveled in three trains of approximately fourteen cars each. Diaghileff and his staff, the twenty or more principal artists, the entire Metropolitan Opera orchestra of one hundred men, two hundred dancers and coryphees, conductors, ballet masters, thirty-six stage hands, and all the supernumeraries, made up the largest and most glittering organization America had ever seen. Every moment of the day (whether enroute, at rehearsal or during a performance) was filled with incidents beyond belief.

Although the members of the company, particularly the coryphees from the ballet schools and theatres of Russia, were a disciplined group, they had no inhibitions in manners and morals. They could not be classed as immoral. They were paganly unmoral in the simple, animal sense of the word. Perhaps their long sojourn in Europe had added to their freedom of life. On board a Pullman train, they slept or dressed, conversed or made love in various degrees of dishabille, and to one who appreciated the perfection of their bodies it was, to say the least, a Sybaritic feast. To the good solid American railway crews, these incomprehensible passengers were something out of an Oriental seraglio, and their ordinary conduct a voluptuous orgy beyond anything their simple imaginations could have conceived. I recall that after leaving Boston, the scene of the first engagement on tour, crews at each division point fought for the privilege of manning our trains, so well had the railway grapevine done its work.

The enormous cost of this unprecedented tour demanded that we give at least one performance each day. For this reason many of our bookings were very closely scheduled. We played a matinee,

NIJINSKY AS PETROUCHKA

for instance, in St. Paul and were to give another the next afternoon in Kansas City. The Chicago & Northwestern Railway did very well with our heavy trains as far as Omaha, but the locomotives provided by the Missouri Pacific to haul us into Kansas City were far too light for our equipment. Due to arrive at ten o'clock in the morning, we pulled into the Kansas City yards at noon. Diaghileff had become very suspicious of electric systems and switchboards in American theatres due to the fact that we were playing great auditoriums, many of which were inadequately equipped. No architect could possibly have had the Diaghileff Ballet in mind when drawing plans for an American auditorium. Before giving a performance, Diaghileff always insisted on a complete scenery and light rehearsal, just to be sure that everything was going to work. In Kansas City we had a special problem. We were booked to play the vast Convention Hall. an oval shaped building without a permanent stage.

25

Therefore, after our late arrival it was necessary to curtain off one end of the great auditorium, install a gridiron on which to hang the scenery, erect a proscenium arch, and hang all of the complicated décor and connect our own portable switchboards and rheostats. Diaghileff insisted that the audience not be admitted until he had completed checking scenery and lights. And it was a rainy day!

The performance was scheduled for 2:15 P. M., the doors to open at 1:00 o'clock. Actually, the doors did not open until 2:30 and the performance began shortly after 3:00 o'clock. As the youngest available member of the staff, I was "selected" to tell the constantly growing audience that the doors would open soon, and to repeat this at ten-minute intervals. In the rain stood hundreds of men and women, not only local residents but people who had come to Kansas City from within a radius of one hundred fifty miles. Patient in the beginning, at each of my announcements, they became more and more uneasy and disturbed. After my fourth appearance, they were vocal in the extreme and it was an ominous, howling mob that greeted my fifth and final bow. Friends said I aged perceptibly that afternoon.

Diaghileff found little to admire in America. He detested our democratic ways, intensely disliked our food and found us crude and unsympathetic. I have often fancied that had he returned to America before his death in 1929, he would have been astonished; for the visit of his Russian Ballet, misunderstood at the time, really had a profound influence on this country. If our direct methods and efficiency annoyed him, we on the other hand had an opportunity to see but little of his most brutal, arrogant characteristics. The management of the tour which was under the general auspices of the Metropolitan Opera Company had been entrusted to an able but cynical showman, Ben Stern. Although Gatti-Casazza, the Italian impresario of the Metropolitan,

was hostile to Diaghileff and his project, Ben Stern made a great effort to keep things on a pleasant and harmonious basis. No effort ever achieved less. As Diaghileff and his company had been brought to America through the offices of Otto H. Kahn, Diaghileff assumed that all of Kahn's subordinates, even those in executive positions, were, as in Russia, menials. He refused to discuss matters with Ben Stern. In fact, he did not acknowledge Stern's existence. As he regarded Gatti-Casazza as his natural enemy, there was only one man whom he recognized. Desiring instructions of even minor importance, Diaghileff always cabled Kahn for advice. And Kahn, during the whole tour, wisely remained in Havana! This brought about unusual tensions and many "incidents," and at times actually threatened the progress of the tour.

One incident stands out in high relief as a symbol of the disunity, suspicion and anxieties which an enterprise of this character can produce. One morning (I believe it was in Cincinnati), Diaghileff came backstage. The scenery for *Cleopâtre* was being struck and the crew was beginning to hang the décor for *Le Carnaval*. Diaghileff and his interpreter were inseparable as he spoke no English. Through this interpreter, Diaghileff gave an imperious command to a busy stagehand and, of course, received no response. Stagehands receive their orders through the heads of their departments whether they be carpenters, electricians or property-men. Diaghileff thereupon struck the worker with his heavy blackthorn stick. I accidentally came upon the scene just as Diaghileff succumbed to the onrush of a dozen outraged men, and I managed to call them off. To the sullen crew I explained that we would have to settle it in some other way and did my best to save Diaghileff's face.

After the performance that night, Diaghileff went as usual to one of the dressing rooms for a conference on the next day's repertoire and cast. This

26

4
NIJINSKY

Nijinsky as man and artist is inscrutable. One can discuss his panther-like stance, the hypnotic poetry of his body in motion, his astounding ability to spring into the air, his seeming emancipation from the laws of gravity, the atavistic cunning of his gestures. Much may be said about his sensitive and impressionable mind. But one had to see Nijinsky to believe the emotions he evoked.

He was the ultimate product of a school, part Slav, part European, matured by his years with the Russian ballet and given curiously oblique slants by a temperament simultaneously bold and retiring; retiring in all his contacts with the world and reality, bold in all his manifestations of the dance. It was a mind, it seemed, pivoted on the outward limits of logic and sanity; a mind which might shift, and did, eventually, into utter unreality.

Nijinsky's European reputation was well known to me as I had read everything available about him. Prepared as I was for a remarkable and awe-inspiring performance there was, nevertheless, something

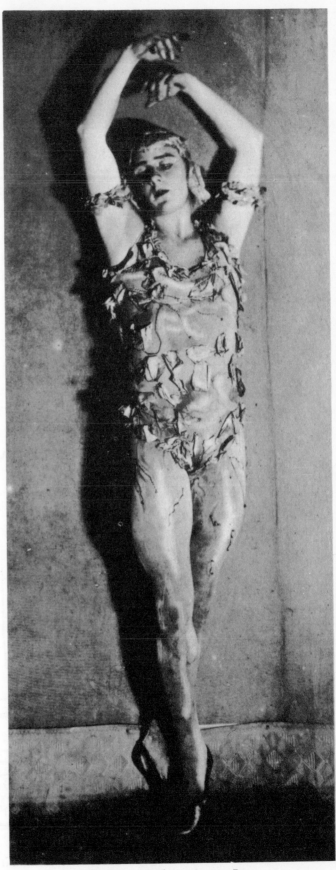

NIJINSKY IN LE SPECTRE DE LA ROSE

meeting was concluded at perhaps one o'clock in the morning and Diaghileff prepared to depart. The huge cavernous stage was in semi-darkness and as Diaghileff strode across it, towards the exit, a chunk of pigiron used in counterbalancing scenery, fell from the gridiron ninety feet above, stripping the rim from the great man's handsome derby. It was an appalling moment. Diaghileff, for all his intellectual courage and daring, was a physical coward and for the next several days he was confined to his special car with a case of nerves. Ben Stern ordered an investigation but on close questioning, no member of the crew knew how or why such a murderous weight of iron could fall from the gridiron of an empty theatre. Fortunately for all concerned, the investigation was allowed to drop.

When Diaghileff died in Venice in 1929, the Ballet Russe had, in a sense, become a European rather than Russian organization, for Diaghileff's experimental seasons had brought such names as Debussy, Ravel, Auric, Satie, Picasso, Poulenc, Matisse, Derain, Milhaud, Cocteau and many other modern creators into his organization as collaborators. Many of Diaghileff's basic ideas are reflected in the ballet organizations now performing annual seasons in America, the most celebrated exponents being Diaghileff's protégés, the remarkable choreographers and dancers, Leonide Massine, Adolph Bolm, Bronislava Nijinska, and George Balanchine. But there never has been anything remotely resembling the twenty years between 1909 and 1929, and the aesthetic revolution which had its healthy repercussions on both sides of the Atlantic was basically the projection of the imagination of one man – Sergei Pavlovitch Diaghileff.

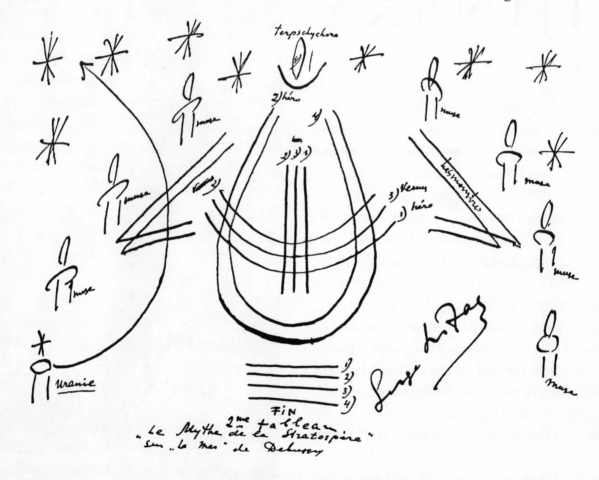

THE FAUN, BY GAUDIER-BRZESKA
[H. S. EDE]

ography a failure, as even Diaghileff believed in 1913? There is considerable evidence that Nijinsky's remarkable inventions to parallel the rhythmic complexities of Stravinsky's score were simply ugly and baffling to a generation steeped in traditional sauvities. His choreography for Strauss' *Tyl Eulenspiegel,* a collaboration with Robert Edmond Jones, created in New York entirely independent of Diaghileff, was not only distinguished, but was prophetic of an interesting new direction. Nijinsky, many believe, was a greater artist as a choreographer than a dancer.

But as a dancer, his place in history is secure. His unparalleled performances in *Giselle, Les Sylphides, Schéhérazade, Spectre de la Rose, Petrouchka, Jeux, Carnaval,* and especially *Le Sacre du Printemps* and *L'Après-midi d'un Faune,* remain unequalled as original conceptions.

In personal contacts he was gentleness itself, and although he was often moody and uncommunica-

DIAGHILEFF AND NIJINSKY, BY JEAN COCTEAU [HASKELL]

of the sublimely endowed acrobat about him which I could never entirely filter out of my consciousness as I watched him dance. Perhaps only in the *L'Après-midi d'un Faune* did he seem to exhibit that inner illumination of the truly great performer — the artist who can physically synchronize his dance mechanism with an entire company and yet endow his personal performance with the revealing essence of the ballet's intent.

There is more than a possibility, however, that Nijinsky had grasped some of the underlying truth of the grammar of movement which in later years was to flower as the modern dance. In retrospect, some of his arbitrary, angular movements which seemed so incongruous against the shimmering curves of the *mise en scène,* those reptilian or animal-like silhouettes, were Nijinsky's own private break with the ballet tradition. Also, the full extent of his capacity as a choreographer is a controversial subject. In the light of contemporary developments in the dance, was his *Le Sacre du Printemps'* chore-

29

tive, his smile was radiant and he had an elusive, feminine charm.

Because of the quarrel with Diaghileff, Nijinsky was not a member of the Diaghileff Ballet Russe on its first American *tournée,* and when the American management decided Nijinsky was necessary to the success of the more extended second tour, Diaghileff retired to Europe. In one sense this proved a great mistake, for Nijinsky was certainly no executive. Indeed, he was already suffering from a mental aberration which later, in its more advanced stage, caused his long confinement.

In one of the cities on the tour, I believe it was in Cleveland, the entire company attended a supper party given in a fashionable suburb. All evening while the guests enjoyed fine food and vintage wines, Nijinsky remained alone. Wearing an old grey suit, a shirt without a collar, and brown unpolished shoes, he sat in a corner seemingly preoccupied with contemplating the two walls. Among the guests at this gay affair was the distinguished pianist, George Copeland, a celebrated Debussy interpreter. At approximately 2:00 A.M. the hostess insisted that he play, and Copeland went to the piano. This was the prelude to an amazing, satyr-like performance. As Copeland began his own arrangements of Debussy's orchestral *L'Après-midi d'un Faune,* out of the corner came the sulking Nijinsky, the movement of his muscles plainly visible despite the comically ill-fitting clothes. The guests drew back and gave him the floor.

It is one thing to see Nijinsky in make-up and costume, aided by the entire *mise en scène* of the Ballet Russe, and quite another to observe him closely in the cruel flat lighting of a drawing room, without a single theatrical accoutrement. Yet, the impossible disadvantages of time and place could not entirely negate. Nijinsky's tremendous powers of communication. When he had finished that poignantly erotic performance, Nijinsky furtively returned to his corner, and without word or gesture resumed his solitary meditation. The guests, greatly moved, departed subdued and silent.

STRAVINSKY 5

Just what Diaghileff's destiny might have been had he not attended a Ziloti concert in 1908 is a subject for speculation. On that portentous night, Diaghileff heard two works, *Feu d'Artifice* and *Scherzo Fantastique,* which aroused such enthusiasm that he insisted on meeting the composer, young Igor Stravinsky. That was possibly the most fruitful meeting in Diaghileff's kaleidoscopic career, for he immediately commissioned Stravinsky to write the music for *L'Oiseau de Feu.*

Diaghileff had been searching for a national ballet, a synthesis of the Russian characteristics, a work which Frenchmen would understand to be *du vrai Russe.* A libretto had been completed by Fokine, Golovin was working on sketches for the décor, and Liadov had been commissioned to write the music. When it was later discovered that Liadov had not written a note Diaghileff fell back on Tcherepnin. But the outline this composer presented was not considered appropriate. Precisely at this period in the development of *L'Oiseau de Feu*, Diaghileff attended the Ziloti concert and heard for the first time the arresting, rhythmic music of Stravinsky, and thereupon a collaboration and friendship began which was to last until Diaghileff's death.

Stravinsky at once became a member of the *Mir Iskustva*, making his first appearance at the home of Alexandre Benois. Although possibly flattered by his acceptance into such distinguished company, it was Stravinsky who would eventually bring the greatest distinction to the accomplishments of the group.

L'Oiseau de Feu was Diaghileff's most important creation of 1910, as it was the first authentic Diaghileff ballet. The music was especially commissioned, and there had been exceptional collaboration between Fokine, Stravinsky and Golovin. The approach adopted in *L'Oiseau de Feu* became standard procedure. One secret of Diaghileff's success rested on a perfect synthesis of music, choreography and décor. No matter how varied the repertoire, Diaghileff insisted that all ballets must be, in a sense, the joint product of choreographer, painter, and composer.

It is interesting to note that the role of *L'Oiseau de Feu* was first offered to Anna Pavlova, who is said to have declined because she disliked the music. In any case, the gulf which finally separated Pavlova and Diaghileff widened. She remained true to the spirit of the Russian classic ballet while Diaghileff continued the creation of a new synthesis, his epoch making experiment which produced the Ballets Russes. The role of *L'Oiseau de Feu* fortunately went to Tamara Karsavina, as her particular talents and remarkable beauty were exactly suited to this choreographic drama.

In 1911 Stravinsky's second ballet, *Petrouchka*, was produced. The basic idea for the score materialized while the composer was at work on *Le Sacre du Printemps*. *Petrouchka* gave Nijinsky an opportunity to demonstrate new facets of his remarkable ability and Karsavina added to her growing fame. Alexandre Benois designed the décor and Fokine the choreography. But it was the music of Stravinsky which gave *Petrouchka* its basic distinction.

Le Sacre du Printemps, the next production, was the result of Stravinsky's intention to construct a primeval ballet and his ideas found a sympathetic collaborator in Nicholas Roerich. The choreography was entrusted to Nijinsky, much to the distress of the composer who realized the dancer's musical shortcomings. Diaghileff planned the premiere of *Le Sacre du Printemps* for the opening of the theatre *Les Champs-Elysées*. Seldom in the history of the theatre has there been an outcry and demonstration such as took place during and following the performance of this work. A smart Parisian audience became a howling mob. Nijinsky had to be forcibly prevented from rushing onto the stage to denounce them. Pandemonium reached such heights that Diaghileff finally ordered the lights off. In a typical attitude and reaction, Comtesse de Pourtales haughtily departed from the theatre, announcing that she would never return if such grotesqueries were repeated. Cosmopolitan Paris was certainly caught off-balance.

In 1917 *Feu d'Artifice,* with décor by Balla, was produced for a tour of sixteen towns in Spain. Two other one-act ballets, *Chant du Rossignol* and *Pulcinella,* were produced in 1920. Massine did the choreography for both works. Décor for *Chant du Rossignol* was by Matisse, while the scenery and costumes for *Pulcinella* were by Picasso. *Le Renard,* a ballet in one act by Stravinsky, was produced in Paris in 1922, as was *Mavra,* Stravinsky's opera, with costumes and décor by Survage.

The next sensationally successful Stravinsky ballet was *Les Noces* produced at the *Gaité-Lyrique* in Paris, 1923. Stravinsky had commenced work on

Les Noces long before the war and had played the first two scenes to Diaghileff in Switzerland as early as 1915. Because of Diaghileff's enthusiasm, Stravinsky dedicated the work to him. Its first performance in Paris was a triumph such as the Ballet Russe had not enjoyed in years. Stravinsky again demonstrated his remarkable gifts by writing a dynamic score for a musical ensemble consisting of a chorus (soloists acting as instruments), four pianos, and percussion. The highly endowed Gontcharova painted the décor, and the choreography was done by Nijinska.

The final Stravinsky ballet to be produced by Diaghileff was *Apollo Musagètes,* performed at His Majesty's Theatre in London in 1928, repeated at the Sarah Bernhardt Theatre in Paris, and later in Brussels. This Helenic opus is in two scenes with décor and costumes by André Bauchant and choreography by Balanchine. Diaghileff had begun to realize that a new generation of artists was developing who were not as sympathetic with his aims as the early collaborators, and during the preparations for *Apollo Musagètes* and his re-association with Stravinsky, something of the old enthusiasm returned. He revealed a new energy as he sought a perfect synthesis of idea and content for this new work. The ballet was a spectacular success and marked the final manifestation of the celebrated Diaghileff character.

These ballets produced under the Diaghileff auspices gave Stravinsky's career terrific momentum. Although his scores were perfect elements for the ballet, they were soon discovered to be even more interesting as programme music, where the listener's whole attention could be devoted to these dynamic conceptions.

It is very late in the day to discuss the pros and cons of the Stravinsky controversy. His earlier works are in the standard repertoires of every symphony orchestra in the world and his ballets remain the pillars of all great companies. Stravinsky, meanwhile, continues to transform himself, to change his musical skin and to emerge with new statements, compact and rich in content. He has an extraordinary faculty for renewing himself, and there is something heroic about his refusal to exploit his past successes.

DRAWING OF STRAVINSKY BY PICASSO

The great public as well as the critics who had been won by the compelling color and sonorities of the earlier Stravinsky works, notably *L'Oiseau de Feu* and *Petrouchka,* have been puzzled by the seeming change which took place about 1924. This, however, was a logical development for a man of the aesthetic integrity and mental capacity of Stravinsky. He had used Russian themes almost to the point of exhaustion, and to repeat himself is not in the Stravinsky character.

This development was toward a concise polyphonic writing, which became discernible in such

33

earlier works as *Les Noces* and *The Fox*. Actually, there has been no break, no "Russian" versus "neo-classic" periods. The musical themes have changed from Russian sources to more universal material, but the structure has remained essentially the same. To understand this fully, one must be familiar with Stravinsky's basic credo. He believes that music is the only possibility by which man may "make stable the category of the present." Meter and rhythm are used as the tools of registration and measurement, devices for providing the image of the present. Stravinsky's unfoldment might be compared to a technician who had developed a very personal but universal method of photographing the visual world as it swings through space. At one time he may employ the amazing colors and exotic forms of the tropics; another time, the austere, profound, but elusive beauty of the desert. The material has changed, but not the technique of creation.

The deeper one penetrates into the phenomena of Stravinsky, the more one fact sets him apart: whereas much great music is essentially literature in which large and small incidents are given an exact musical equivalent, Stravinsky stands, in contrast, as a creator of aesthetic entities which have an existence wholly independent of their programme and stories. That which was considered formless before him, he has found to be form. His later work is not a return to Bach. The discerning will perceive that he has returned only to the structural organization which, in one of its manifestations, flowered as Bach.

In other words, Stravinsky has gone back to fundamentals, just as painting, lost in a morass of sentiment and other elements foreign to the basis of art, purged itself through cubism, with a return to such basic elements as the cylinder, the cube and the cone. Stravinsky knows that music is not an element through which we express our emotions, describe our environment, or state our moral concepts. Rather, it is the one domain where man may realize the present and where he can command the elements of sound and time. Regardless of the popular success of his earlier works, it is a strong possibility that Stravinsky's eventual place in musical history will rest upon his later, more perfectly balanced accomplishments.

Perspicacious observers realize that Stravinsky did not, in the conventional sense, write dances. *Les Noces* is a cantata. *Le Sacre du Printemps* is a symphonic poem. *Petrouchka* is a composition in classic style. In *Pulcinella* we rediscover the characters of the *Commedia dell'Arte*. All maintain their musical integrity.

It may seem strange that Stravinsky, early in his career, should have felt so constantly drawn to the stage. But the limits imposed by the theatre seem to have favored his development. Stravinsky used the ballet as a challenge, and solved his problems within and despite limitations. As a result, the most completely pantomimic music yet devised for the theatre is more effective in concert than on the stage!

6
PAVLOVA

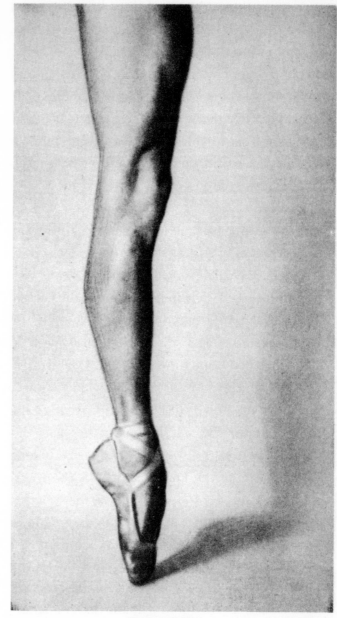

PAVLOVA'S FOOT

Pavlova was a pioneer, not the aesthetic pioneer of new ballet horizons, but the torch bearer who took the spirit of the Ballets Russes to a large part of this civilized globe. The Diaghileff Ballet Russe made two tours of North America and two tours of South America. Apart from these its amazing twenty years (1909-29) were spent in Europe and the British Isles. Pavlova and her company, on the other hand, consistently repeated seasons in Europe, in North and South America, and in other parts of the world. Her husband, Victor Dandré, once remarked to me that at least one-half of Pavlova's life for a period of twenty-five years had been spent on steamships and trains; and certainly the only homes she knew were hotel suites.

It takes conviction amounting to a religion to pursue a career which means a daily encounter with the vicissitudes of cold and drafty theatres, the impersonality of hotel rooms, uncertain railway schedules and uncomfortable trains; and in addition the irritations caused by audiences which often completely misunderstand your purpose, to say nothing of the obtuseness of reviewers.

Anna Pavlova did have sustaining pillars of strength, some visible, others completely unsuspected. She was deeply rooted in the classic ballet, she had known the expanding ballet world of Fokine, she had been the dancing partner of Nijinsky, and Diaghileff had enthusiastically pronounced her the greatest ballerina in the world. Added to this, she had a sense of her own inherent desire to spread the message of the dance. The devoted Dandré was

35

as understanding and as faithful as a life companion should be. And she was remarkably fortunate, throughout most of her touring days, in her selection of managers. Max Rabinoff, who took Pavlova around the world, was a man of understanding. He fully appreciated the quality of his star and her company; he was sensitively capable of interpreting her art to the new world; and he was a shrewd businessman. These are the qualities which make the perfect impresario.

Pavlova came to America with Mordkin, and in the larger cities of America their triumph was complete. America had never seen anything like the Pavlova of those days. She did not dance — she floated. Pavlova was lyric poetry in motion. Mordkin, on the other hand, was a fiery, virile dancer with an Adonis-like body, and the combination was irresistible. The success of Mordkin disclosed in Pavlova a quality not unknown to actresses, movie-stars and prima donnas — she was jealous of her partner's success. There was always humorous speculation among those "in the know" as to Pavlova's next dancing partner, for too much success meant a new name in the program. Some of the dancers must have suffered from psychological vertigo — the dancing partner of the incomparable Pavlova this month, next month consigned to oblivion! The *Swan* was a woman of iron will and determination.

The private lives and personal characteristics of most admired actors, dancers or musicians are very likely to be disillusioning to the layman, and this is largely the layman's fault. The possession of a great dance technique, a superb voice or acting ability, is not necessarily mated to great humanistic qualities. But the public wants its idols to transcend the pitfalls common to us all. The star is expected to be Saint or Salome, or more exciting still, a paradoxical blend of both.

This idealism leads to unnecessary disappointments. The sophisticated person will ask of performers neither violence in their virtues nor splendor in their sins. He accepts, often with amusement, their frequent humanness, their vanity, and their pettiness. Off-stage, the greatest performing artist is seldom important. The illusion evoked while on the stage is the highest reality most of them attain.

The gossamer-like Pavlova of *The Gavotte, The Glow Worm*, and the *Swan* was admired by millions on three continents. But she had qualities unknown to her great public. Backstage she was a strict disciplinarian, often a tyrant. She and her company worked straight through until dinner time, as lunch would usually consist of sandwiches or other trifles brought to the theatre. Following dinner, the hour preceding the performance was devoted to "warming up." Inclusive of the performance itself, this meant a day of fourteen violent, exhausting hours. But no one ever attained the stand-

ANNA PAVLOVA

ards Pavlova had set for herself and her company. Often she would slap each member of her company resoundingly as they came offstage for not meeting explicitly her highest aims. And this despite the applause ringing in their ears.

A case in point which I well remember: Hilda, a featured dancer, came offstage during a New York engagement with the audience thundering an ovation. Pavlova, a grotesque figure without make-up, wearing a soiled kimona, had secretly observed the finale of her solo dance. Furious at some slight infringement of technique, Pavlova quickly approached the girl and gave her a vicious slap in the face. Hilda naturally burst into tears as the other members of the company gathered comfortingly around, hoping to restore her equilibrium. The insistent applause continued. Pavlova, who had returned to her dressing room, was aware of it. Sensing the situation she rushed on stage, embraced the sobbing Hilda and kissed her warmly, rearranged her make-up and pushed her smartly back upon the stage.

After several American tours, Pavlova began to understand America and the value of team work, or what we call cooperation. She even sensed the value of the newspapers in creating opinion favorable to her, and during our final year of association, she allowed me to make advertising arrangements with manufacturers of fine automobiles. This was the precursor of the testimonial sort of identification which was later to become commonplace. Those were pioneering days difficult for this generation to understand. Dancing was even frowned upon in many homes, and it was only the more sophisticated public which attended the ballet.

About this time Pavlova discovered the American cafeteria. Often she took the entire company to these palaces-of-the-tray, and never could resist sampling from the dishes selected by every member. Next to dancing, Pavlova's passion was good food in surprising quantities. She was the despair of dining car stewards on every famous train. Usually, when there was an opportunity, I wired those stewards in advance enabling them to stock up on supplies!

Pavlova toured constantly, believing the intelligent American public would sooner or later respond to the enchantments of ballet, as they certainly did. But in those early tours, in many cities, the engagements were wretchedly attended. Indeed, fifty percent of the performances did not pay expenses, so that the profits of the larger and more appreciative centers were exhausted in deficits. It was not until her last two or three American tours that she had a public solidly and numerically strong, and an audience which truly responded to her very superior offerings.

Now she can be seen in true perspective. Pavlova is a great legend, a goddess of the dance, a continuous and perpetual idol, a challenge to every ballerina now dancing and to those to come.

St. DENIS

7

In our concept of space and time, a potential force may be compared to the growth of a tree. An idea takes root and grows steadily upwards as many personalities join forces. At a certain time or point, the various divergent ideas (the branches) begin to separate and go their individual ways, with each limb numbering its adherents (twigs and leaves) by the thousands.

Isadora Duncan and Ruth St. Denis, at approxi-mately the same period in American adolescence, were motivated by an identical force. As each ma-tured, we see that two definite branches of dance concept grew from these divergent personalities. Moreover, each was basically the product of that nebulous word mysticism.

If Isadora's mysticism exulted in the body, in freedom from the trappings of costume and dress, as well as emancipation of the mind and the passions, then it must be said that Ruth St. Denis conceived of it as a sublimating influence. Through the dance Ruth St. Denis would escape passion and enter the world of free and pure spirit. Both of these ideas apparently produced a maximum of personal suffering, self-analysis, and frustration.

As John Martin has pointed out, every great era in the development of the dance has produced parallel characters and a division along somewhat comparable lines. He appropriately cites Camargo and Sallé in the 18th Century; and in the 19th, Taglioni and Elssler, who divided an art between them in a substantially similar manner.

St. Denis was a contradiction. She took the Orient as her text but her dances were anything but Oriental. They became characterizations or pictures of the Orient, arabesques perhaps, having little or nothing to do with the intrinsic significance of Oriental dancing.

Much of the Denishawn material, verbal and printed, which has come into my hands stems from Ramiel McGehee, who was associated with Ruth St. Denis for many seasons. His descriptions of the torments of the flesh and the spirit to which St. Denis subjected herself are apocalyptical; she was to a remarkable degree a house divided against itself.

The great St. Denis *pièce de résistance* was the now storied *Radha, a Hindu Temple Dance*. To arrive at this pretentious exhibition, St. Denis ransacked public and private libraries all over the United States, talked and studied with East Indian dancers, Oriental art dealers, Swamis, pseudo Oriental performers whose stamping ground was Coney Island, and carried on prodigious studies in theosophy and Egyptian antiquity. But *Radha* launched Ruth St. Denis on an astonishing career of not only fifteen hundred performances, but to fame on both sides of the Atlantic. And this achievement was anything but mystical!

In 1914 St. Denis married her dancing partner, the youthful Ted Shawn, and no estimate, however casual or superficial, may be made of Ruth St. Denis without immediately contemplating him. This man of great energy and undeniable gifts was certainly equally responsible for the celebrity of Denishawn. Ted Shawn undoubtedly needed the established St. Denis as much as she needed his youthful enthusiasm and ideas, and it is safe to say that both grew remarkably through their long association.

Shawn accepted the underlying qualities of St. Denis as a dancer, a woman of the theatre, and a romantic with mystical tendencies. But if Shawn shared St. Denis' admiration for the Orient and the Yogis of the East, he leaned rather more towards the liberated ideas of Walt Whitman and Havelock Ellis, balancing the Bhagavad-Gita with the Occident.

Oriental and Occidental literature and religions (plus a mixture of the primitive when they at last

TED SHAWN

39

TED SHAWN IN FLAMENCO DANCES

encountered the Navajos) were the motivation of Denishawn. Their dance was a synthesis of the classic ballet technique, the dances of the Orient, and what is known as "character" dances, and they were performed before provincial and cultivated audiences all over the world with equal success.

Denishawn, for several years, was a vogue of great and interesting proportions.

Without minimizing the influence which these two semi-pioneers had upon our incipient understanding of the dance, it is possible that the most important result of the St. Denis-Ted Shawn col-

ST. DENIS IN EAST INDIAN NAUTCH

laboration was a by-product. Out of this anomaly, this curiously confused mixture of the Orient and the Occident, the sacred and profane, came that vital new generation of dance personalities and dominant influences – Martha Graham, Doris Humphrey, Charles Weidman, and a host of other lesser artists all over the United States.

McGehee and I often speculated upon the effect this new crop of protégés had upon St. Denis and her curiously blended orthodoxy, observing that she must have greeted the emancipated Martha Graham with the incredulity of a hen staring at the broken egg which produced a swan or even a peacock!

But Ruth St. Denis and Ted Shawn cannot be dismissed as negligible contributors in the development of the dance. They carried the torch in a period of groping and uncertainty which may have been the guiding light for hundreds of unknowns, as indeed it was for those who emerged triumphant from what Ted Shawn has so liberally and honestly called the Denishawn environment – "this school of free, individual dancing." After all, it was a period of imitation. Photographers were attempting to make photographs resemble etchings and engravings, printers were copying William Morris, the engravers were paraphrasing painters, and all of us were aping Europe or the Orient. Out of this maze of conflict and false starts and confusion, Ruth St. Denis and Ted Shawn gave the dance an important rejuvenation, and they succeeded in giving personally honest performances despite material which had no inherent destination.

41

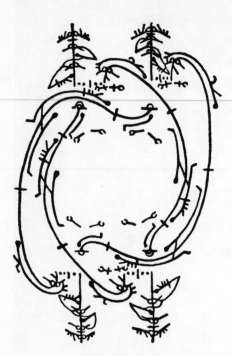

CHOREOGRAPHIC NOTATION. CLASSIC BALLET

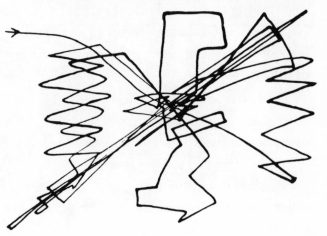

CHOREOGRAPHIC NOTATION, MODERN DANCE (Arch Lauterer)

8
CHOREOGRAPHY

Choreography is both the least understood and the most important element in dance performance. Choreography is dance design. It might well be called the anatomy of the ballet, or the means by which the movements of performers are given unity, cohesion and significance.

The roots of choreography are deep in unrecorded history. We know that ancient priests in expressing the solemn ecstasy of worship, carefully designed their dignified movements or dances, and these men were possibly the first choreographers.

With the Renaissance, dancing, dormant throughout the Dark Ages, was accepted and approved in Italy as an important element in the elaborate theatrical projects with which the great families entertained themselves and their guests. Since that period, dancing has never been absent from the world's stage.

The ballet of today is a synthesis, a story motivated by dancing, settings, costumes and music. This cosmopolitan art is the product of writers, painters, composers, designers, dancers, and chore-

42

ographers. Paralleling most developments, the ballet has traveled a very long road to reach its present complex and highly organized state. Music, painting and ballet were first sustained by kings and courts, and ballet, performed only by men, was an exclusive and elegant entertainment.

Although the amateur ballet was brought to France by Catherine de' Medici, and Louis XIV danced in his own ballet, the dance did not reach professional status until past the middle of the 17th Century, when for the first time women were admitted as performers. From Taglioni, to Duncan, Nijinska and Graham, women have been equally responsible for important reforms and extensions of the art.

The first revolution occurred in the 18th Century when Camargo discarded the whalebone bodices, towering coiffures and other ridiculous and inhibiting equipment and adopted something akin to the present ballerina's tights, carefully camouflaged by skirts. Noverre, one of the great historical choreographers, built his ballets around a story. Forecasting a more comprehensive future, he gave it point and created the ballet of action.

Tzar Alexis brought the Italian ballet to Russia late in the 17th Century, and Peter the Great was responsible for the Court ballets. But it was Tzarina Anne who founded what was to become the traditional Russian ballet by establishing a State supported Ballet School and importing a French *maitre de ballet* to provide discipline and character.

For many years the ballet in Russia maintained its Italian flavor and traditions, and during the reign of Nicholas the First, the great romantic dancer Marie Taglioni was brought to St. Petersburg for command performances. From 1858 to approximately 1910 Marius Petipa, the celebrated *maitre de ballet,* ruled the Maryinsky Theatre with a stern and classic hand. It was not until after the beginning of the 20th Century that revolution again transformed the classic ballet. With the advent of Isadora Duncan and her "new freedom," Michael Fokine was impelled to proceed with his arresting innovations and reforms.

This chapter will deal with but five important choreographers who have made ballet history — individuals who have shaped the ballet and who, together with the brilliant Bronislava Nijinska, are largely responsible for its present form, vitality and life.

The conflicting claims of the ballet and the modern dance have led to endless confusion and misunderstanding. Ballet and the modern dance flourish side by side. If the ballet ceases to make intelligible statements it will gradually lose its audience. If the modern dance is a vital consistent development it will inevitably gain new followers and a larger audience. The line of demarcation is in attitude. The ballet creates its illusion through stylized repetition of forms and movements, presenting aesthetic appeal made directly to the emotions. The modern dance employs the raw materials of life itself to create an illusion of reality, an appeal directed to the emotions through the intellect. Both attitudes demand a sound structure for complete fulfillment of intention. It is the choreographer's responsibility to supply the blue-print and the physical framework which makes the illusion possible.

The four men and one woman we are about to consider are celebrated for their contributions to ballet. But in justice it must be said that they have frequently employed the basic principles of the modern dance and have often ventured far from the confines of the classic attitude.

FOKINE

Some dance authorities maintain there has never been a revolution in the ballet. They call it evolution. Their explanation is that ballet has periodically been rescued from decay by vigorous reformers who have swept away meaningless clichés and given the classic tradition a wider scope and a new freedom. There is much truth in this. The Italian classic ballet underwent very decided changes when transplanted to Russian soil. Again, it flowered with new vigor and hitherto unknown and gorgeous blossoms when Diaghileff took his Ballets Russes to western Europe. We are witnessing a similar chameleon-like change as youthful Amer-

MICHAEL FOKINE

icans pick up the classic threads—the Ballet Theatre being the spectacular example. Revolution or evolution (it is a matter of semantics), the most revitalizing force for the classic ballet in our time has certainly been Michael Fokine.

Fokine not only gave the classic ballet a new direction, but he actually resuscitated an art. For outside of Russia, ballet had become but a quaint survival of sentimental memories evoked by former ballerinas, a kind of palsied habit, or an opera interlude.

Fokine took violent issue with the reactionaries who maintained that "things have always been thus and so, and so they must always continue." The appearance of Isadora Duncan was a tremendous encouragement. It was a confirmation of the conclusions and convictions at which Fokine had independently arrived. If Isadora was changing the prevailing ballet theories, Fokine was equipped by knowledge and temperament to instigate the changes within the existing framework. Duncan would base her revolution on an emotional upheaval which would sweep all before it; but Fokine realized the necessity of a more practical approach, that of using the material at hand, of transforming old instruments with new techniques and, more important, he realized that the dancer's entire body is the true instrument of the ballet.

The career of Michael Fokine must be considered in relation to his time. This first dancer of the Maryinsky Theatre before World War I, first dancing partner of Pavlova, and inspired choreographer, was a man of invention, conviction and courage. Even without the unprecedented opportunities presented by Diaghileff, Fokine would have left his mark on the ballet of our time. His long list of creations include *Le Pavillon d'Armide, L'Oiseau de Feu, Petrouchka, Thamar, Schéhérezade, Le Coq d'Or, Le Dieu Bleu, Paginini, Spectre de la Rose, Bluebeard, Papillons, Carnaval, Prince Igor, Cleopâtre, Narcisse, Daphnis et Chloe, Sylphides,* and many other choreographic dramas. Many of these are vital and compelling works when seen today, although it must be understood that no contemporary ballet company produces them with the integrity of Fokine's original conceptions. However, many of the Fokine works have achieved a classic stature, and will, therefore, be standard in ballet repertoire. His activities in America never remotely equaled his great accomplishments in Russia or with the Russian ballet in western Europe, although he achieved a certain nostalgic distinction with several works for the Ballet Theatre. But the contributions of Fokine place him decidedly in the great tradition of Vigano and Noverre. The impetus he gave to the dance made it one of the most vigorous and vital expressions of the early 20th Century.

BOLM

If the classic ballet were an indigenous American expression, with roots deep in our consciousness, we would have great permanent organizations independent of the ephemeral touring companies. Assuming the possession of such ballet assets were a reality, Adolph Bolm would certainly be the head of one or all of them. For Adolph Bolm is a rare phenomenon among dancers and choreographers – he has the executive mind.

Bolm has understood the American spirit perhaps better than any foreign-born dancer or choreographer. Moreover, he has made full use of American material, and has become part of the American scene.

He was born at St. Petersburg, his father being a first violinist and conductor at the Mikhailovsky Theatre. At the age of ten he was accepted at the Imperial Ballet School, gaining the first prize when he graduated in 1904. Immediately, he was transferred to the Imperial Ballet at the Maryinsky Theatre. There, he quickly established himself through his brilliant dancing, his ability to mime, and his natural sense of the theatre. He traveled throughout Europe visiting museums and attending operatic and ballet performances, and studied for a time under the great Maestro Enrico Cecchetti in Italy.

His executive ability received its first practical experience when he organized a ballet group which toured the Scandinavian countries and north central Europe. His *prima ballerina* was Anna Pavlova, as celebrated in Russia as she was unknown outside its borders. It was on this expedition that the people of Prague expressed their complete acclaim by filling the stage with flowers at the final performance, dragging Pavlova's and Bolm's carriages from the theatre to the station, and decking the locomotive with garlands.

The success of Bolm's little organization became the talk of Europe and entrepreneurs in Paris in-

ADOLPH BOLM

vited Bolm to bring his company to the French capital. Thereupon, Bolm exercised his rare managerial judgment and declined. He knew Diaghileff's plans for the following season, and soundly understood the necessity of Pavlova and Bolm making their debuts in the world's most fastidious city under the proper auspices.

At the beginning of World War I in 1914, Bolm, who was in Switzerland, received an invitation to stage a season of ballets in London. Sir Oswald Stoll contemplated a season with Karsavina as *ballerina* and with Bakst acting as artistic collaborator. But simultaneous with this offer Diaghi-

45

leff also arrived at Lausanne. Diaghileff had just received an invitation from Otto H. Kahn, Chairman of the Board of the Metropolitan Opera Company, to bring the entire Ballet Russe to America for a season in New York and an extended tour. Bolm was invited to join him. Almost immediately it was discovered that neither Karsavina, Fokine, nor Nijinsky could make the contemplated American tour. Bolm, therefore, accepted the dual responsibility of *premier danseur* and choreographer. This meant that he also assumed the herculean task of rehearsing the company in a repertoire of twenty ballets. This was complicated by the fact that because of the war, many regular members of the company were unable to join the group in Switzerland and there were many new dancers in the organization. The fact that America saw the Diaghileff Ballet with its character unimpaired is largely due to the prodigious efforts of Bolm.

Following the first American tour, Diaghileff took the company to Spain and it was during this period that Bolm composed a ballet to Rimsky-Korsakov's tone-poem, *Sadko,* with costumes and décors by Gontcharova.

As plans began to take shape for the second American tour, the American management insisted on the appearance of Nijinsky. Because of the Diaghileff-Nijinsky misunderstanding, it was obvious that if Nijinsky joined the company, Diaghileff would retire. Bolm, apprehensive of a successful tour without the steadying, experienced influence of Diaghileff, hesitated to join the company for its extended coast-to-coast American *tournée.* Diaghileff urged him to go for the good of the company, and Bolm finally capitulated. The second American tour of the Diaghileff Ballet proved that Bolm's judgment had been correct – the company lacked the full Diaghileff flavor. Mid-way in the tour, Bolm was injured, and after hospitalization, elected to remain in New York rather than rejoin the company. Almost immediately he organized the Adolph Bolm Ballet Intime, consisting of twelve dancers, including such Oriental artists as Roshanara and Michio Ito.

Bolm's remarkable abilities as a choreographer began to flower in America. His production of Rimsky-Korsakov's *Le Coq d'Or* at the Metropolitan Opera House was in the finest tradition, as was *Petrouchka* which followed later for the same organization. For the Chicago Opera Company in 1919, Bolm created the choreography for John Alden Carpenter's *Birthday of the Infanta* with scenery and costumes by Robert Edmond Jones. Bolm took his Ballet Intime to London for a successful season at the Coliseum in 1920 and on his return to New York devised a wholly new type of ballet using the jazz medium, based on Herriman's cartoons of *Krazy Kat,* with music by Carpenter. For the following two years Bolm was the *maitre de ballet* of the Chicago Civic Opera, and never before or since has the ballet of that company been so important or exhibited such style.

The Chicago Allied Arts under Bolm's choreographic direction was for a time the most significant ballet organization in America. Special ballets were composed and several modern works were designed to music by Debussy, Ravel, Erik Satie, Stravinsky and Alexandre Tansman. Henri Eichheim's *The Chinese Legend,* Vaughn Williams' *Christmas Carol,* Clemente Herscher's *The Farce du Pont Neuf,* were given their first American performances. It was during this prolific period that Bolm introduced Tamara Karsavina to Chicago audiences. Shortly thereafter he created the world premiere of Stravinsky's *Apollo Musagètes* for the Elizabeth Sprague Coolidge Chamber Music Festival, with costumes and décors by Remisoff. Brought to Hollywood to produce a ballet for *The Mad*

46

Genius, Bolm gave an augmented version before huge audiences in the Hollywood Bowl as *Le Ballet Mecanique.* For the San Francisco Opera Association, he designed an entirely new version of Rimsky-Korsakov's *Le Coq d'Or,* again collaborating with Remisoff, and in addition, choreographed a number of new works including *Patterns* to music by Tcherepnin.

In 1941 the Hollywood Bowl Association engaged Bolm to recreate choreography for Stravinsky's *Firebird Suite* with décor and costumes by Remisoff. Among the novel features of this production, the orchestra was placed on the stage concealed by decorative screens and the dancers occupied the huge area between the stage and the audience. Bolm created choreography on a large scale, using dance figurations which carried the meaning of this choreographic drama to the farthest seat in the huge amphitheatre. That same year the Ballet Theatre invited Bolm to stage Prokofieff's *Peter and the Wolf* for the initial performance of that new organization at the Rockefeller Center Theatre with décors and costumes by Lucinda Ballard.

For the 1945-46 season of the Ballet Theatre *L'Oiseau de Feu* was produced for the first time by that organization with new choreography by Bolm for which Stravinsky augmented the original *Firebird Suite.* During all these years of choreography, Bolm continued his career as a dancer.

Diaghileff once said that a choreographer must be a man of culture. Bolm is not only a man of culture, but he has been particularly sensitive to the complexities of this period of transition. The seed he has sown throughout America has provided, and will continue to provide, a rich harvest for many generations of dancers.

MASSINE

When Diaghileff reached across the space-time dimensions of Europe and Russia to cast a seventeen-

LEONIDE MASSINE

year-old student in the role of Joseph in Strauss' *Legende de Joseph,* he demonstrated the quality of perspicacity which distinguished his entire career. The handsome young Leonide Massine could not have been discovered at a more fortunate time, nor could his versatile abilities have been more vital to the future of Diaghileff.

Europe was in the midst of a cruel war. Nijinsky's departure for South America was the sad beginning of the end. Fokine and Nijinska were unavailable. Diaghileff was without a balletmaster. His need for a dancer and a choreographer was obvious, but even more imperative was his need of a man who could assist in guiding the organization in a new direction.

47

The extraordinary diligence and skill of the great Cecchetti raised the brilliant Massine from the *corps de ballet* to a *premier danseur* in a few months. But it was Diaghileff's unerring judgment and daring which insisted upon an important role in Paris and London for a novice juxtaposed against the background of a magnificent company. And London and Paris immediately confirmed Diaghileff's wisdom. Massine was an emphatic success. Although a solid beginning had been recorded, both Massine and Diaghileff were aware of the metamorphosis which must take place before such acclaim was completely deserved. The training of Massine as both dancer and choreographer proceeded with increased intensity.

The success of Massine in *Joseph* which had seemed so vital at the moment was the least contribution this youth made to the Diaghileff plans. Massine's mind and temperament were both admirably poised for the forthcoming Diaghileff venture into the *School of Paris* thought and attitude. He set the key that determined the future productions of the organization.

With Massine, the new concepts of art already claiming the world's attention through the works of Picasso, Matisse, Derain, Gris, Braque, Cocteau, Satie, and Stravinsky were assimilated and incorporated by this amazingly versatile ballet organization. Whereas the synthesis of music, dance, dècor and plot constituted the anatomy of former Diaghileff ballets, Massine supplied a new choreographic conception, and proceeded to evoke the poetic-aesthetic atmosphere of a now historic period.

The first complete escape from the clichés of the ballet was undoubtedly the Jean Cocteau-Erik Satie-Leonide Massine *Parade* which was first produced in 1917. Stripped to its most telling essentials, it was in a sense a forerunner of the mood and attitude later adopted by first the dadaists, and then the surrealists.

The abrupt change from the lush and lavish productions of Bakst and Rimsky-Korsakov to such a brittle oddity as *Parade* was too much for Paris. But it indicated a turning point, and at least a portion of the *Parade* innovation survived in later successes.

The rest of the story is history. Leonide Massine has few counterparts. This artist is undoubtedly the purest extension into this day of the Diaghileff tradition and attitude, and to it he has added his own individual dance comment as a choreographer extraordinary.

From the early *Soleil de Nuit* to *Union Pacific* is an enormous span, which embraces more choreographic structures than can be credited to any single designer. The list which comes to mind, certainly incomplete, includes such accomplishments as: *Les Matelots, Pas d'Acier, Ode, Seventh Symphony, Bacchanale, Symphony Fantastique, Le Bal, Beach, Le Beau Danube, Boutique Fantastique, Cappricio Espagnol, Choreartium, Contes Russes, Les Fâcheux, Good Humored Ladies, Gaité Parisienne, Les Présages, Pulcinella, Rouge et Noir, Sacre du Printemps, Aleko, St. Francis,* and *The Three Cornered Hat.*

BALANCHINE

The precocious brilliance of George Balanchine has developed choreographic results of a very high order. The mature Balanchine is possibly the classic ballet's most able and versatile designer.

In 1925, Balanchine, at the age of twenty-one, designed Igor Stravinsky's *Le Rossignol,* with décor by Henri Matisse; and this was presented in Paris by Diaghileff. Previous to leaving Russia in 1924, Balanchine had choreographed a number of works including *Waltzes* by Ravel, *General March* by Chopin, *Boeuf Sur le Toit* by Milhaud, *Enigma* by Arensky, *Salome* by Strauss, *Pulcinella* by Stravinsky, and several other productions for the State Opera.

Following this unprecedented youthful performance the growth of Balanchine since the Diaghileff debut has been steady and consistent. As his own horizons have deepened and broadened, he has gained in power and control of his medium, and his inventiveness is remarkable.

There have been several shifts in attitude and style. Recognized as a classicist in the Diaghileff days, his choreography by 1932 had begun to reveal significant changes, many of which were indicative of his present manner.

For the past several years, Balanchine's choreography has moved in the direction of the *natural momentum of a figure in motion;* and even though its intentions and destination is not that of the modern dance, certain fundamentals are related. It is a return, in a sense, to authentic classic dancing — the classic world of Petipa-Ivanov in that it is based on dancing of movement, not the various arts of story-telling mimicry, rhythmic rubato, or distortion of the human figure. And Balanchine's own simple but profound statement that "a ballet may contain a story, but the visual spectacle, not the story, is the essential element," should be displayed in upper case type at the beginning of every printed ballet program.

In this old-new pursuit of dance qualities, Balanchine is on particularly solid ground. He is working with the natural rhythms of the body, and in concert with the laws of physics. His ability to create highly unforeseen dance sequences is unified with the dancer's natural movements, and the results are often startling in their purity. It is a highly expressive technique which adds exhilaration and variety to both the solo and the group dances.

My experience in witnessing Balanchine ballets includes *The Card Party,* with music by Igor Stravinsky, presented by the American Ballet in New York; *Danses Concertantes* also by Stravinsky and with décor by Eugene Berman, presented by the Ballet Russe de Monte Carlo; his ballets in the Broadway productions of *I Married An Angel;* and *The Song of Norway.*

These performances can only be characterized as brilliant. In manner they seemed to possess an originality remarkable even in this day of sophisticated virtuosity. Even in such theatrical banalities

GEORGE BALANCHINE

as *The Song of Norway,* this natural rhythmic flow subjected to Balanchine's unerring sense of invention, produces a sense of vitality which raises the entire production. The collaborations with Stravinsky seemed especially worthy of companionship with the electrically alive scores of this prodigiously inventive composer. The Broadway productions were miles above the usual trite or pretentious ballets associated with musicals for far too many seasons. They were so good that one wished for

49

a less cosmopolitan element from his admittedly compelling choreography. It would be interesting to observe, for instance, Balanchine's reaction and response to witnessing a season of Navajo Indian ceremonial dances!

But my knowledge of the Balanchine repertoire and its various accomplishments is sketchy. I want to augment this chapter with the opinions of a dancer and choreographer, a dance critic, and a dance authority, respectively. They are excerpts from articles appearing in the February-March 1945 issue of Dance Index.

Agnes de Mille writing of Balanchine's choreography in 1930:

"One of the roughest of these dances and by far the most effective is the love duet performed by Doubrowska and Lifar in *The Prodigal Son,* a ballet produced by Diaghileff for the first time in London last July. Doubrowska, as an ancient Biblical courtesan, full of splendor and wickedness, hangs against the Prodigal's body, her arms locked over his bent elbows, her wrists dangling, her long slender legs bent so that her toes trail in the air, her knees moving slowly in rhythm with his steps. He crosses the stage languorously under this sensual burden. She sits before him and with frenzied strength jumps to her toes. He wraps her about his waist like a belt (a variation of the trick made famous years ago by Mitti and Tillio) and with feet spread apart watches her slide down his body to the ground where she lies in a coil, hand clutching ankle, spine tense as a sprung trap. He sits beside her, swings toward her, away from her, tries to lift himself from the floor, sinks back, and twists into her arms in an inextricable tangle. This scene constitutes one of the most important seductions to be found on any modern stage."

"Aside from the subject matter of the returned wanderer, which has been important for approximately two thousand years, the method of treatment is worth noticing as a useful development of the adagio. For the same reason less athletic themes and their treatment should be considered. Happily

adagio lends itself to subtleties as well. Imaginative concepts hitherto seldom expressed except with words, the moods and imagery that words connote, can be wrought into visual form by the same hackneyed acrobatic stunts. It is with vigorous wiles that the courtesan lures the Prodigal into her power, as we have seen, and vigorously she makes known her triumph. Her attendants immediately smother him in her crimson train. She mounts to the shoulders of one of them and stands looking down a good ten feet at her subdued lover. In this device, a tumbling trick, Doubrowska opens up an entirely new field for theatrical expression. Literally she towers over her prey. No actress by voice or presence could dominate the situation more completely."

Edwin Denby writing in 1945:

"Balanchine in these new animated, constantly shifting, plotless and unneurotic pieces by stressing the dancer's impetus makes one follow a dance performance with consistent interest without drawing your attention to familiar unhappiness. You don't watch the dance to see if the dancers come up to an emotion you expect beforehand, you watch to see what they do, and their variety in animation exhilarates; you are interested without knowing how to label the emotion. And so you are not tempted to excuse your pleasure, or rationalize it, or appreciate it mentally. I think that this direct enjoyment of dancing as an activity is the central aspect of ballet style that Balanchine has rediscovered. As in the new style the dancer is no longer divided between divergent impulses of motion, and as there is no longer a conflict for precedence between dancer and choreographer, so there is as you watch no painful split of emotion between your social consciousness and your dance pleasure. These classic and free pleasures of peace are as great as those of a tortured romantic disorder. They offer us a new emotion one is eager to enjoy."

Lincoln Kirstein:

"George Balanchine, to anyone upon whom dancing exercises its enchantment, must always seem the sorcerer, different in scope and scale from other contemporary choreographers. His best works are all classical, and though he can compose for the individual dancer better than anyone else in the Western world, his ballets are created apart from the dancers who appear in them and they can be given a new interpretation by a notable talent fortunate enough to perform them. Every season Balanchine feels that he has discovered a wonderful new dancer, because, as dancing is his magic, he is continually bewitched by the possibilities of a new body which even itself may not yet feel either strong or secure, but which he can see projected through time into a powerful interpreter."

"Balanchine was not always a popular choreographer with the public. When *Serenade* was first performed eleven years ago, it seemed almost too simple from the hands of a man who was then supposedly capable of only the perverse and peculiar. Yet, how many ballets of that year can be revived today and retain their freshness and purity as it does? Or as *Apollo, Mozartiana,* and *Ballet Imperial* do?"

"These classical ballets will serve as the base for future repertoires much as the works of Petipa and Ivanov have served in the past. The next generation will use Balanchine's work as a standard for style and asymmetrical extension, the grand contemporary academy of the development of the capabilities of the human body on the largest possible scale."

DE MILLE

Neither Doris Humphrey's passionate search for truth in a world governed by equilibrium, nor Charles Weidman's stunning researches in the contemporary American idiom, nor Martha Graham's penetrating analysis and hypnotic projection of the human soul, nor George Balanchine's sardonic abstractions and amazing inventions are entirely absent in the very American forces and ideas which motivate Agnes de Mille.

From a pseudo intellectual background tinged with the philosophy of Henry George, a young spirit singularly unwarped by powerful Hollywood influences, a talent given point and polish by Continental experience, Agnes de Mille emerged

AGNES DE MILLE

from the status of an intelligent but uninspired dancer into a provocative and often sharply original choreographer.

Three Virgins and a Devil, Black Ritual, Tally Ho, and other works for the Ballet Theatre somehow failed to register as emphatically as have her choreographic contributions to Broadway productions. By returning to the indigenous spirit of Lynn Riggs' *Green Grow the Lilacs,* Agnes de Mille lifted the Theatre Guild's production of the fabulously successful *Oklahoma* safely above the routine formula of the typical musical show. Even more specifically was this true in the case of *Bloomer Girl.* Several first night critics thought her Civil War ballet the best thing in the show; and time has proved those reactions to be correct. As for the Theatre Guild's *Carousel,* although the producers were satisfied with her ballet which came late in the second act, Miss de Mille was not. After convincing Oscar Hammerstein, who wrote the

DRAWING BY PICASSO (1923 Programme, Ballet Russe)

book and lyrics, that there was room for improvement, she reconceived the ballet and revised more than a third of it before the big musical had its second performance.

These and many other demonstrations have given her a solid position among present day choreographers, and it is likely that the perspective of time, plus future productions, will heighten her contribution. In any case, her blend of intelligence, inventive facility, and a natural understanding of balanced movement have provided Broadway with some of its most diverting and surprising moments.

KIRSTEIN

9

Lincoln Kirstein is not a dancer, or a professional critic, or a manager in the accepted sense. Although he has written an indispensable book, *Dance,* and a discerning pamphlet, *Blast at Ballet,* he does not pose as a writer. But Lincoln Kirstein is something of all the above, and more. By temperament, training, education and some bitter experience, he is the most articulate and penetrating spokesman for a steadily emerging dance consciousness to be found on either side of the Atlantic.

Kirstein's preoccupation with the later productions of Diaghileff in his association with the *School of Paris,* was one of honest fascination. "Social-satire, American jazz, the everyday vacation and boulevard life of the nineteen-twenties;

dada, neoclassicism, the falsely naïve, the falsely archaic, the decorative folk-lore no longer of Russia, but now of England, Italy, France or Spain," and the other accomplishments and caprices of Diaghileff's later inventions were evaluated by him at their true worth. Back in America he proceeded on the theory that *classic ballet* must not, either in practice or in an audience mind, be confused with *Russian ballet.* For Kirstein the ballet is a form of artistic expression just as the symphony is a form of musical expression. A Tschaikowsky, a César Frank and a Beethoven each may write a symphony, yet each maintains its Russian, French and German characteristics. And, so, he believes, should the ballet, a form of dance expression which is flexible enough to accommodate the Italian, the Russian and the American character. It is a logical viewpoint, and one can find no fault with it until we examine the contemporary trends.

But this in no way dims the Kirstein contribution. Faced with an almost impenetrable jungle composed of balletomane, commercial dance-manager, giddy female "sponsor," white-Russian prejudice, and a public high-pressured into believing that ballet means Ballet Russe, Kirstein has proceeded along his constructive way. He remains the one important independent operator of a ballet school and a ballet company, and ballet's most courageous and perspicacious writer.

His failures have been magnificent. The very lack of success which his American Ballet experienced in its association with the Metropolitan Opera Company is its most telling Medal of Merit. His successes, such as the Ballet Caravan, were a clean break with the clichés of the Ballets Russes; his school is the best in America. *Dance* is the most scholarly and original book yet written on that subject; his *Blast at Ballet* has given heart to more than one discouraged organization, and to thousands of individuals disillusioned by the prevalent managerial system.

His influence has been felt through the American Ballet, the sponsoring of George Balanchine, the School of American Ballet, and *The Dance Index*. Many modern dancers (Erick Hawkins, Merce Cunningham and Dorothy Bird come to mind) have worked for long periods at the Kirstein school.

In time, it may be seen that Lincoln Kirstein did not give full and proper importance to dance expressions operating outside the orbit of the classic ballet, that he was too close to the scene and too immersed in the surface waves to be fully conscious of the great ground swells of the middle 20th Century. But that does not in the least negate his valuable championing of our most talented young performers, or of his immense contribution in opening the eyes of America to its own dance possibilities. He is a friend of thousands whom he will never see or know.

DRAWING OF MARTHA GRAHAM BY CHARLOTTE TROWBRIDGE

GRAHAM

10

Few enterprises are as presumptuous as attempts to estimate a contemporary revolution. Its very immediacy makes evaluation difficult.

Three bonafide revolutionary experiences have taken place for me since I have been conscious of the world of arts. I was twenty years of age when the impact of the Armory Show struck me in 1913. The cubistic pictures of Juan Gris, Picasso, Braque, and other painters of the *School of Paris* did not, in my estimation, seem distorted fantasies of patho-

logical minds, as many critics and all the Sunday supplement writers assured us, but rather exhibits curiously parallel with life. It was obvious to me that these men were far from the crazy anarchists they were thought to be. How could they infuse elements such as paint on canvas, with such arrestingly powerful overtones? It was not their insanity which overpowered me; it was their sanity and their complete lack of inhibitions.

Looking at these same pictures today, I can smile

LOUIS HORST, MUSICAL COLLABORATOR

at my first reaction. They read as impellingly alive and rich as other old masters; they are now well known and very interesting friends.

My second awakening was the International Composers Guild. Edgar Varèse founded this organization as a vehicle for the presentation of works of living composers. At the Varèse concerts I heard for the first time the works of Schoenberg, Satie, Honegger, Milhaud, Toch, Krenek, Ravel, Varèse and the later works of Stravinsky. Today, rather than radical, these works seem to me inevitable.

The third revolution came as abruptly as the others. There was a young American girl, a Martha Graham, who had induced a lively controversy, and Doris Humphrey and Charles Weidman were being mentioned as extraordinary. I was as unimpressed as I was disinterested.

Then arrived the night when Martha Graham came upon the stage and began a performance so knowing, and so communicative, so daringly articulate, that I was utterly exhausted after her first number and even considered leaving the theatre. I wanted time to think, to rationalize, to be sure I had actually witnessed such an astounding performance.

Since that time I have seen yearly performances of Martha Graham and her company, have managed many of them, and have published a book on this new concept of the dance. The mere fact that a dancer and choreographer could continue to invent and create over a sixteen-year period and never repeat herself is amazing enough, but to continue to infuse each performance with the tension and the primordial freshness of spring, is an accomplishment unparalleled in my experience. For thirty-five years I have known the theatre from both sides of the footlights, but a Martha Graham performance continues to be, for me, the only theatrical exhibit not composed of old material newly presented, or new material offered in old forms.

Martha Graham would be the first to deny credit for the so-called modern dance. Doris Humphrey is a very sensitive and original artist; Charles Weidman is a prolific creator of dance design and a great artist as a performer; and there are many new and vital personalities in the rapidly expanding fabric of the modern dance tapestry. But Martha Graham's influence on the modern dance transcends even the impetus Isadora Duncan gave the dance world twenty-five years ago. For the modern dance is not an extension of the classic ballet; it is a new language of dancing, bringing with it almost limitless possibilities of communication.

I have the greatest respect for tradition, but believe that certain forms are overworked and empty, and when they are perpetuated they tend to draw the spirit of the dance back into periods of the past which have no identification with today.

56

That states, as well as I can express it, my attitude regarding the classic ballet versus the modern dance. If we are interested in yesterday's atmosphere, ideas, and emotions, the classic ballet is one of the greatest museums available, and this is not said as either sarcasm or criticism. If approached as one would approach an exhibition of old masters, or as one would listen to Beethoven or Tschaikowsky or Ravel at a symphony concert, there are certain ballet performances which will stand seeing year after year.

But I am not one who believes the contemporary world will be wholly or successfully expressed by the mechanism of the classic ballet. I have seen very popular performances (*Billy the Kid, Filling Station, Fancy Free*) of contemporary material presented in the ballet formula. For me, it is simply not a complete success. There is a residue of classic ballet inherent in such performances which inhibits a full and free communication of the spirit of our day. That is an honest statement with which a majority will agree. If Kandinsky, for instance, were to use representational or recognizable forms in his pictures, they would immediately lose their compelling communication, would be freighted with an element alien to his intentions.

The very technique of the classic ballet is this alien element, this opaque element which gets in the way of a completely transparent presentation of idea-content.

The Martha Graham repertoire is rapidly becoming a tradition. There will soon be revivals, as indeed there should be. And on the list of Martha Graham creations which deserve to be seen again are *Primitive Mysteries, Integrals, Frontier, Horizons, Appalachian Spring* and *Imperial Gesture*. These will serve to keep the current Graham audience aware of the milestones in the development of the modern dance. Graham has investigated the science and the language of motion as has no other dancer or choreographer. Her imagination

MARTHA GRAHAM BY EDWARD BIBERMAN

frequently conjures forms which seem foreign to plastic realization, yet by force of conviction, plus an amazing technique, they become highly communicable. A Martha Graham rehearsal is a laboratory experiment, and here one learns that perfection is agonizingly unattainable. These rehearsals are far removed from the routines and the mannerisms of the ballet. They are, in effect, a clearing house where the whole anatomy of communication is dissected, where every possible avenue is explored, then put through its trials and accepted or rejected on the basis of its integrity and acceptability in the language of motion.

57

DRAWING BY CHARLOTTE TROWBRIDGE

There are moments in Martha Graham's dancing when the poignant meaning is projected with the velocity of a pitched ball; again, she is introspectively powerful, reflecting rather than projecting. The undanced portions of her choreography are not emptiness, but carefully considered elements of construction. She shares with the painters and composers of this generation a passion for condensation. Seeing her in action is to realize the vast difference between highly trained talent and something close to genius.

Martha Graham has elected her own direction. Her singleness of purpose and her devotion to the dance is the result of fanatical integrity, privations, ridicule, and physical exhaustion. Crystallized in her dance is an essentially American character.

But this American character is also her passport to universal communication; she speaks directly and eloquently to every human being whose mind is open to the possibilities of a new day. Hers is a great voice in the sense of an Edward Weston, a Paul Klee, or an Igor Stravinsky. And, as Martha Graham recedes into history, her accomplishments will certainly be understood as one of the truly significant forces of the 20th Century.

THE ALBUM

This section is divided into three groups: *The Ballet, Modern Dance,* and *Portraits and Persons.* The first twelve photographs were taken by Victor Jessen from the audience while the ballet was in performance. No attempt has been made to include all the contemporary ballet dancers or all those comprising the modern group. *Portraits and Persons* includes many photographs, now rare, collected over a period of more than thirty years. Viewed today, some are funny, some are even ridiculous; others are historical documents, and still others are irreplaceable. Your own conditioning and point of view will determine your reaction. One fact is a certainty: here are the people who carried the torch.

The Ballet

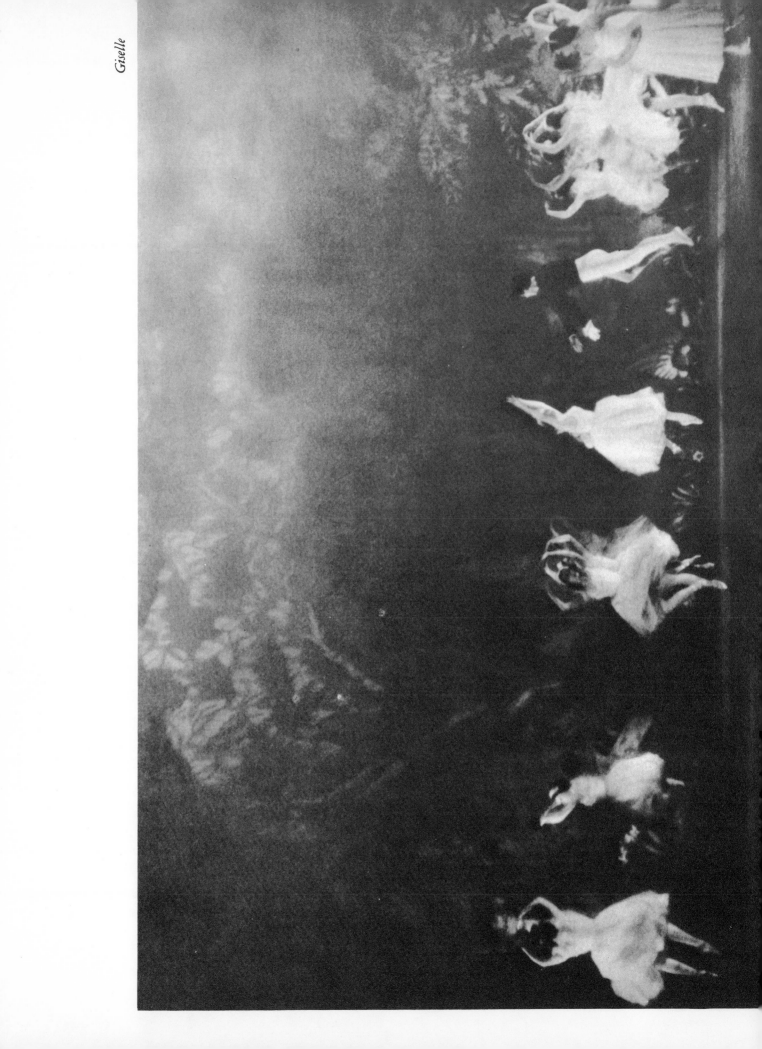

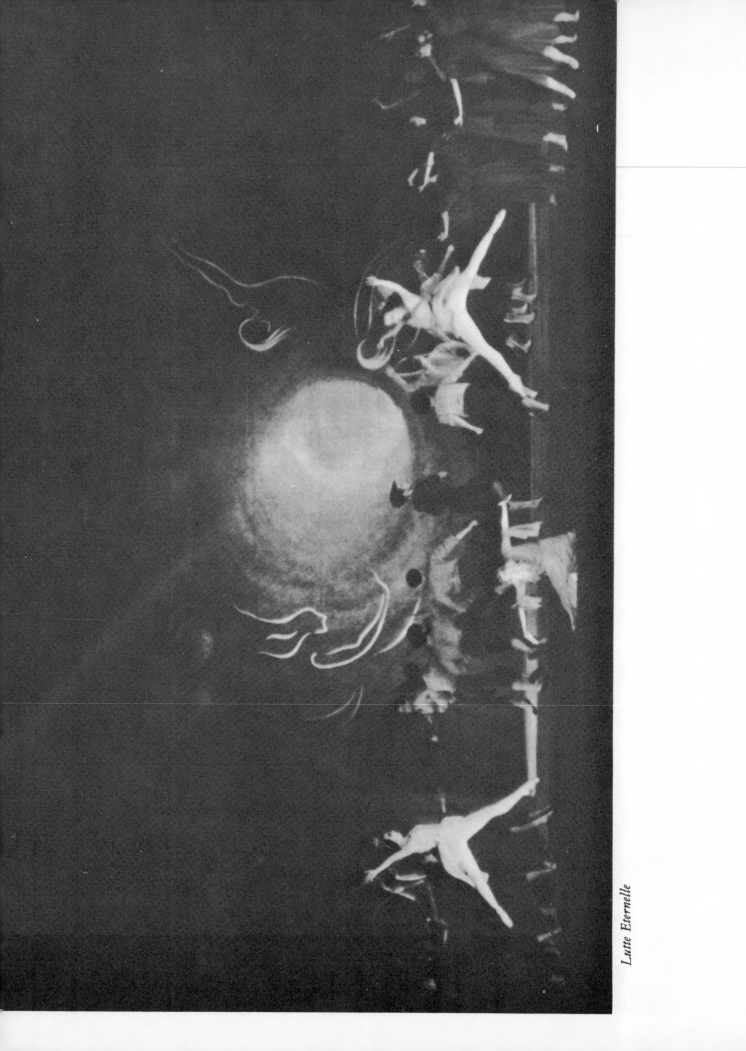

Lutte Eternelle

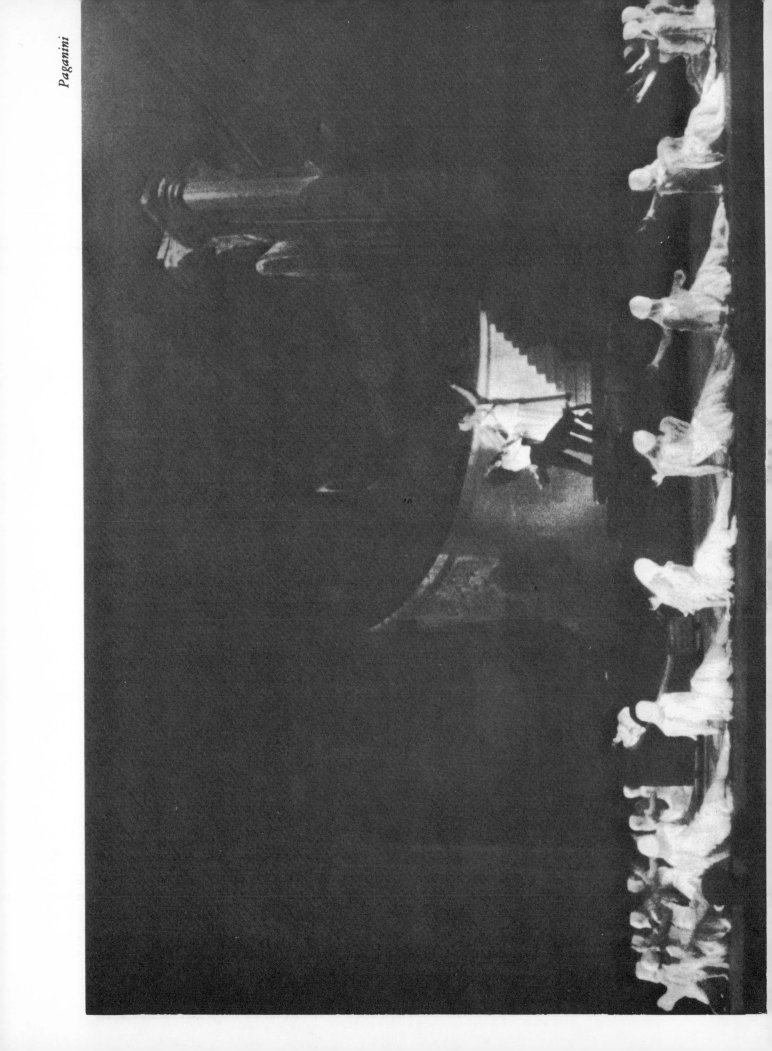

Paganini

Graduation Ball

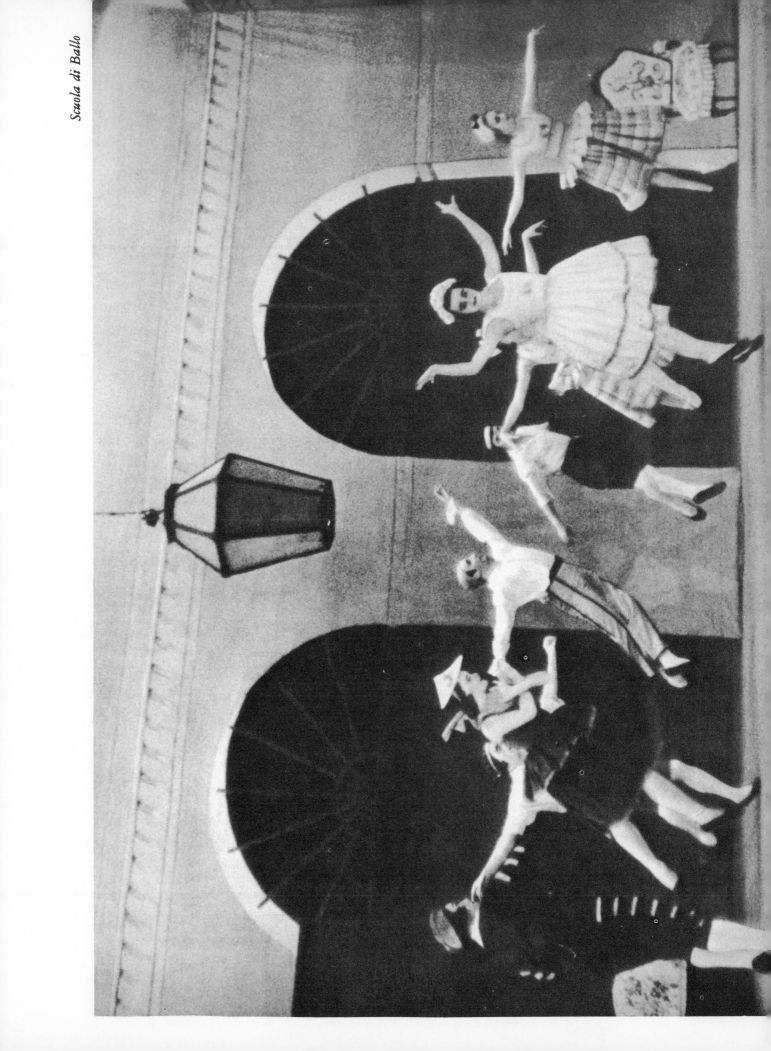

Devil's Holiday

The Seventh Symphony

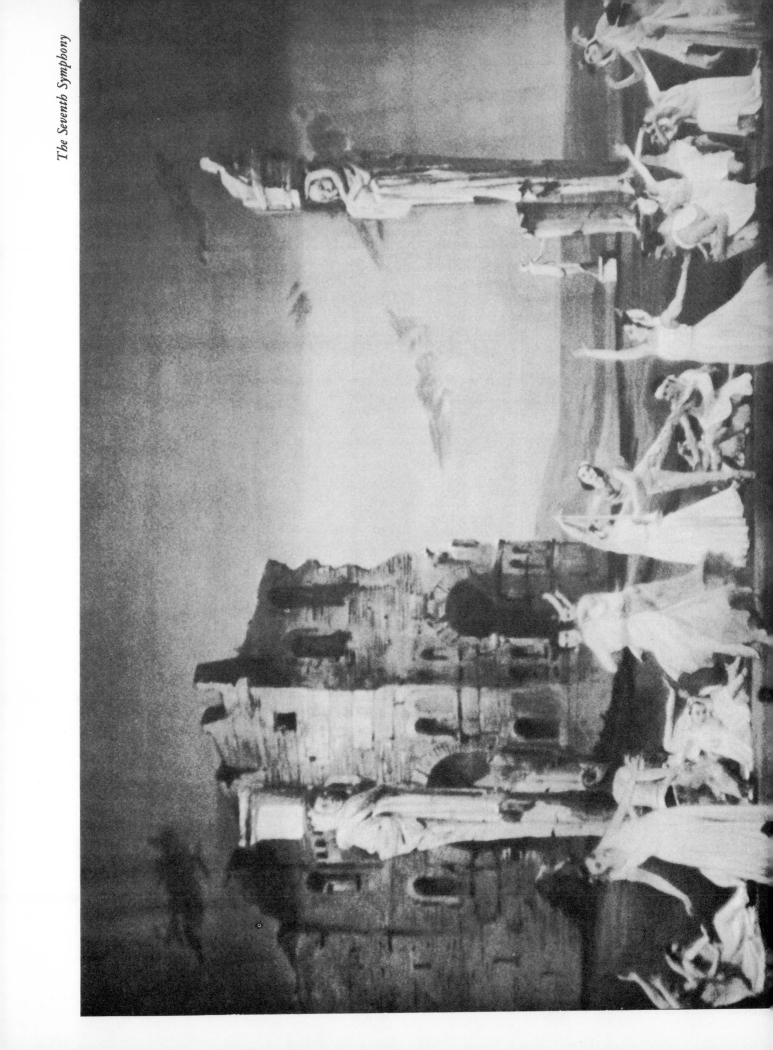

Les Sylphides

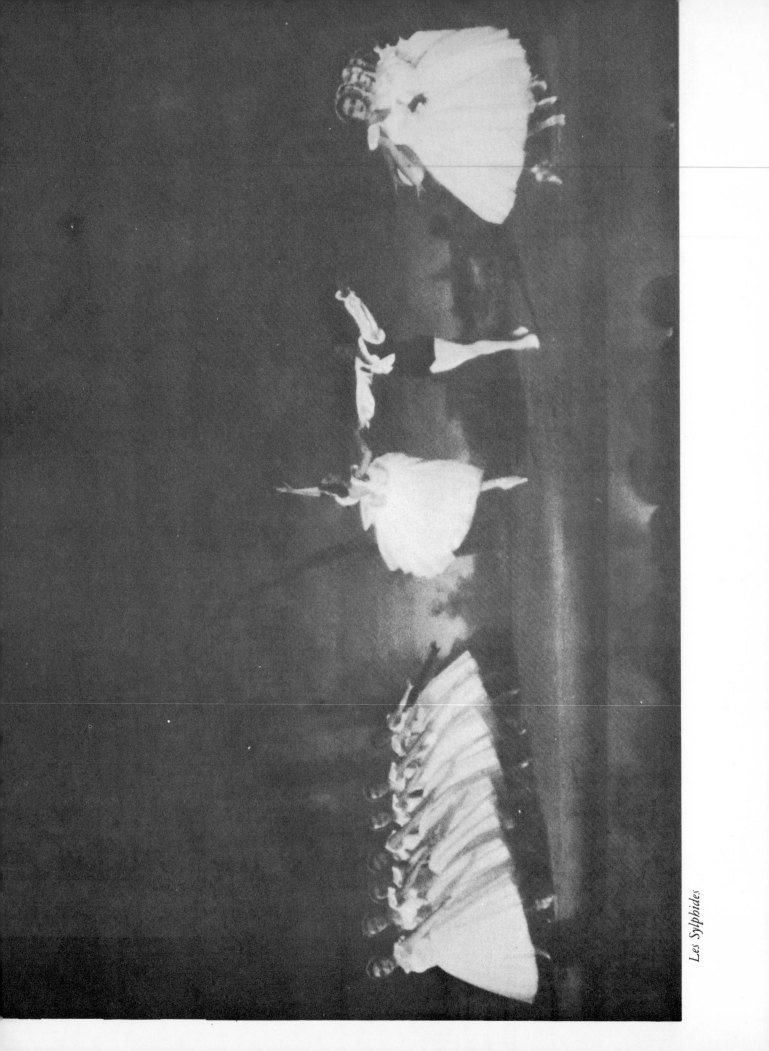

Les Sylphides

ALICIA MARKOVA

IRINA BARONOVA   NANA GOLLNER
NORA KAYE   LUCIA CHASE

MICHAEL KIDD
PAUL PETROFF

JEROME ROBBINS
ANDRE EGLEVSKY

IGOR YOUSKEVITCH

ALICIA MARKOVA AND ANTON DOLIN

LEONIDE MASSINE

George Balanchine

DAVID LICHINE

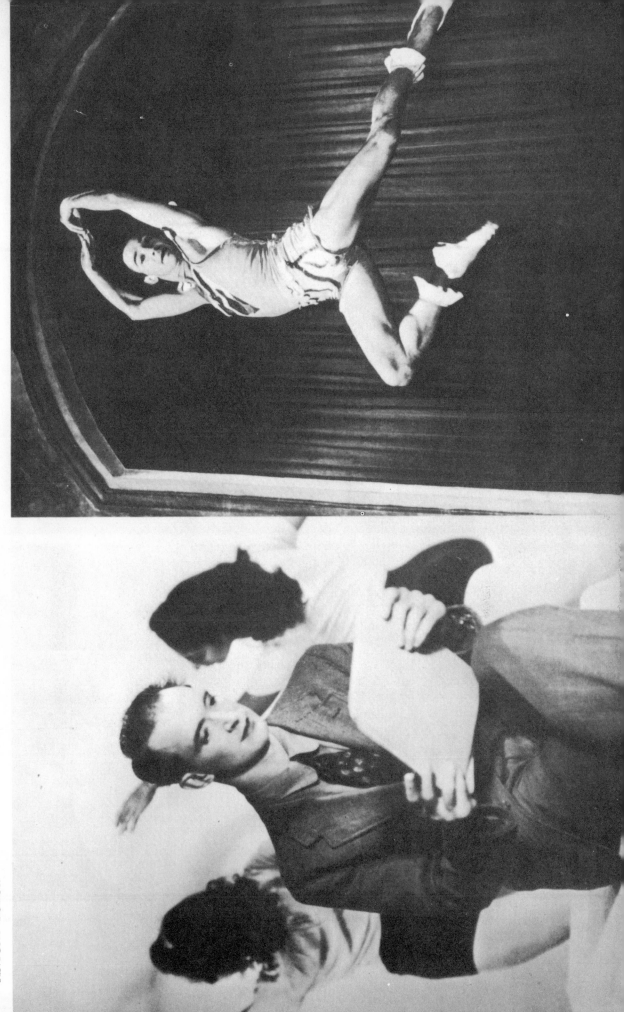

ANTONY TUDOR

NATHALIE KRASSOVSKA

MIA SLAVENSKA

IRINA BARONOVA

ANTONY TUDOR AND EUGENE LORING

Modern Dance

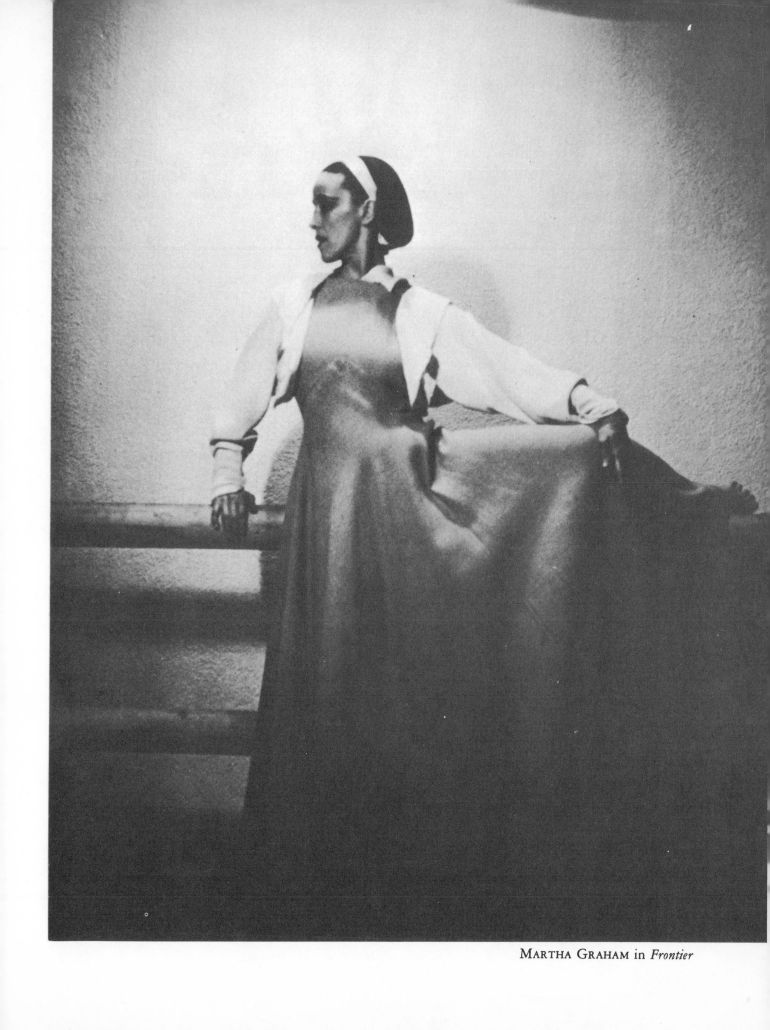

MARTHA GRAHAM in *Frontier*

MARTHA GRAHAM AND COMPANY in *American Provincials*

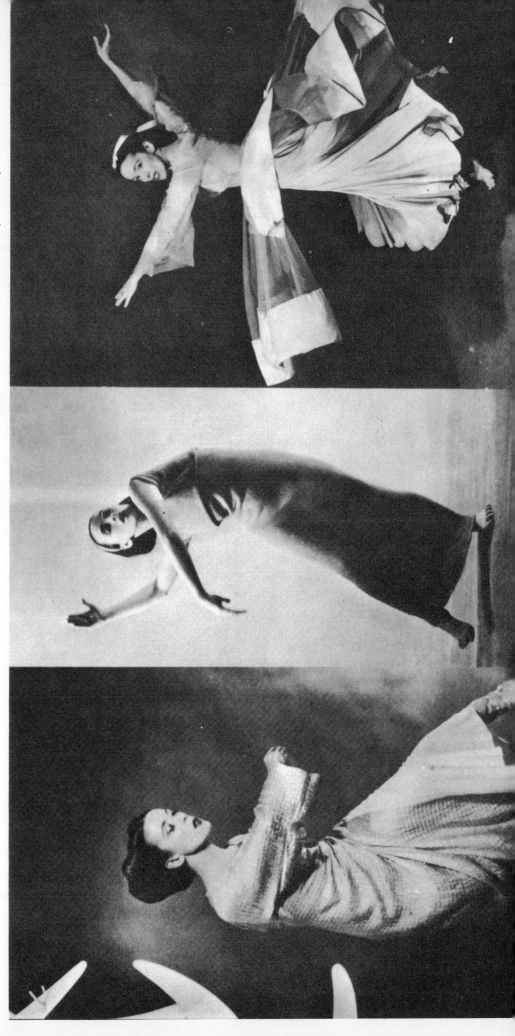

MARTHA GRAHAM in *Herodiade*, *Ekstasis*, and *Letter to the World*

MARTHA GRAHAM AND COMPANY in *Appalachian Spring*

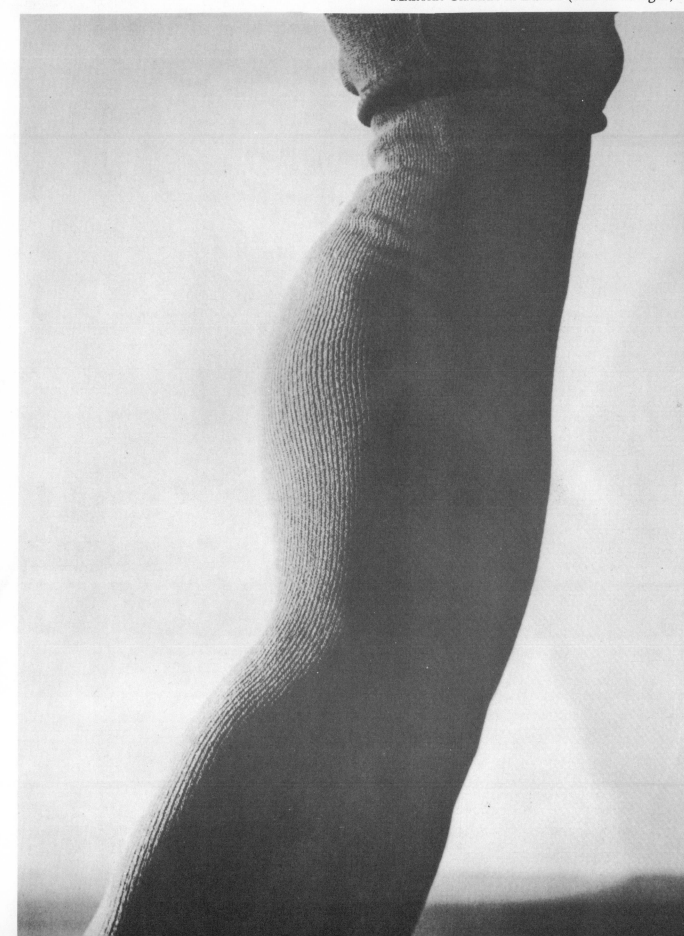

Martha Graham in *Sarabande*

Vicente Escudero (Enlarged Contact Print by Edward Weston)

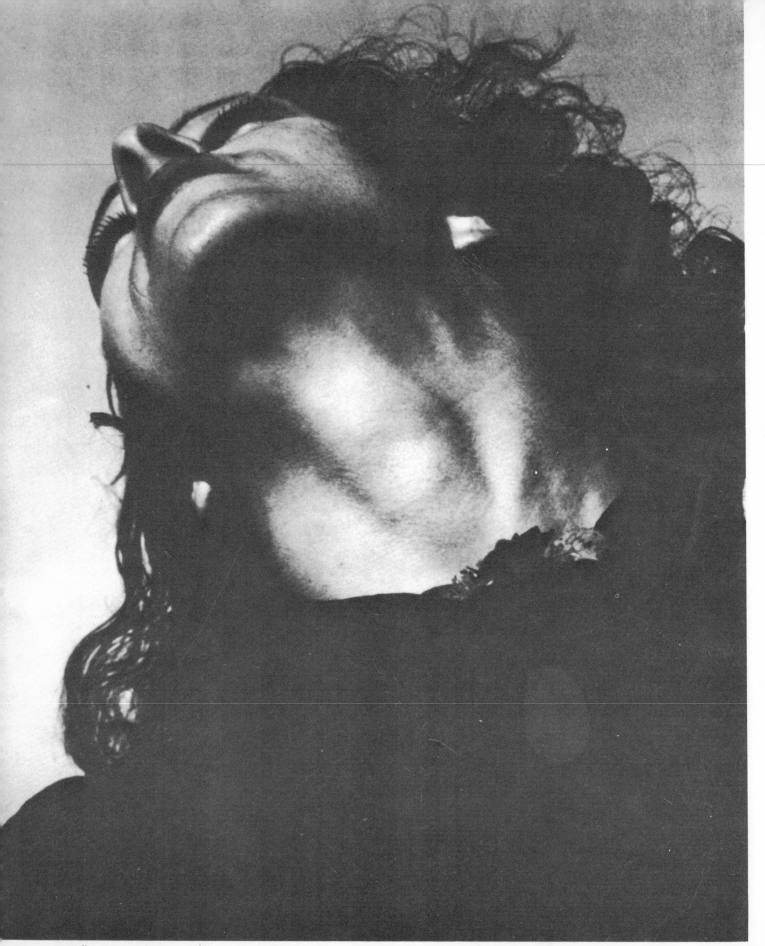

TERESINA (by Edward Weston)

HARALD KREUTZBERG

IRIS MABRY

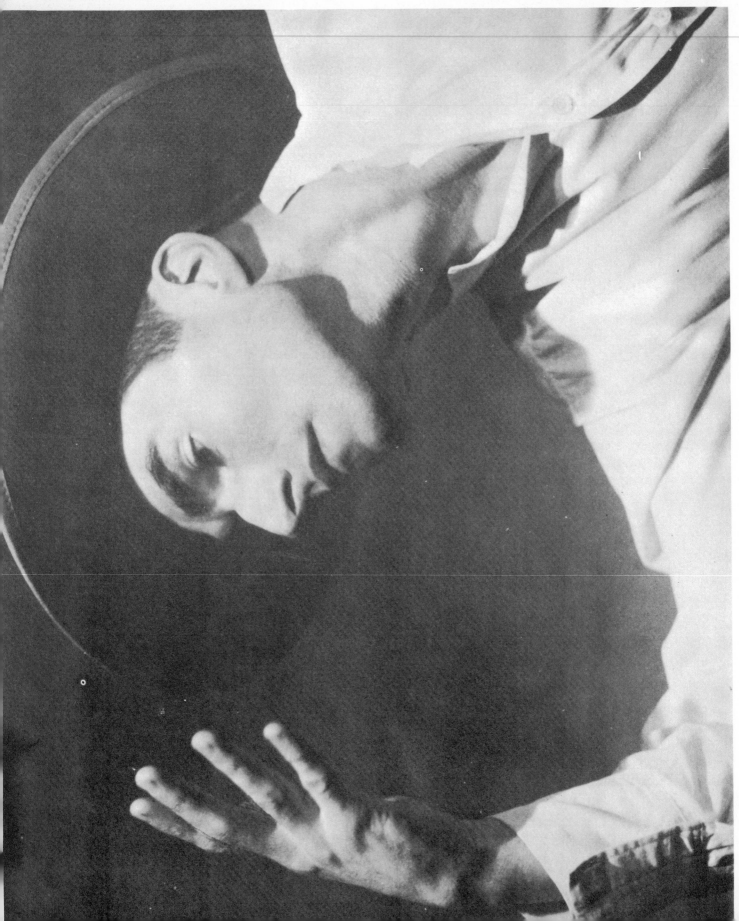

VALERIE BETTIS (Barbara Morgan)

MERCE CUNNINGHAM

Taos Horse Tail Dance

JOSE LIMON

AGNES DE MILLE (Carl Van Vechten)

AGNES DE MILLE in *Rodeo*

CARMELITA MARACCI (Lansing Brown)

1946

Thank you, Merle, for your deep understanding and friendship.
Carmelita

CARMELITA MARACCI in *Viva tu Madre* (Gjon Mili)

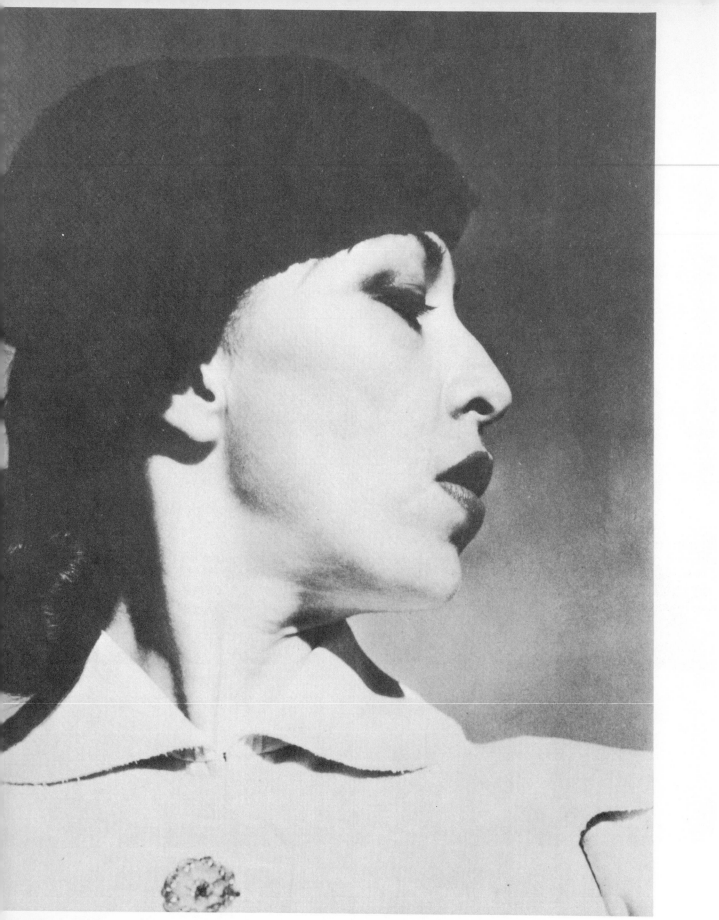

CARMELITA MARACCI (Enlarged from a Print by Edward Weston)

To
Merle Armitage
Mary Wigman

MARY WIGMAN

DORIS HUMPHREY (Gerda Peterich)

Doris Humphrey in *The Matriarch*

Doris Humphrey—Charles Weidman Group in *Lynchtown*

CHARLES WEIDMAN (Gerda Peterich)

Portraits and Persons

ISADORA DUNCAN (Museum of Modern Art, Dance Archives)

ISADORA DUNCAN in *Marseillaise* by Arnold Genthe (Library of Congress)

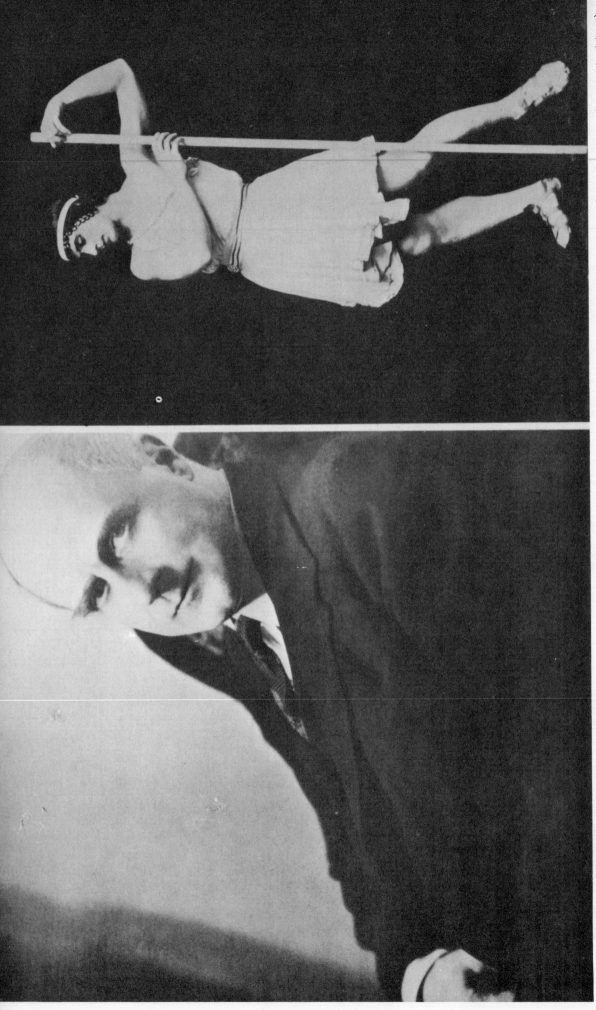

MICHAEL FOKINE (Museum of Modern Art, Dance Archives)

MICHAEL FOKINE (Ballet Theatre)

TAMARA KARSAVINA (Merle Armitage Collection)

Portrait of Leon Bakst (From: The Decorative Art of Leon Bakst, Courtesy of the Fine Art Society, London)

Portrait of Diaghileff by V. Serov (Merle Armitage Collection)

THE DIAGHILEFF BALLET RUSSE Trains Depart from Chicago, 1916

L to R: Bolm. Grigorieff. Massine. Sokolova. Buick. Diaghileff. Lopokova. Tshernisheva. Khokhloon. Picasso.

Below: Merle Armitage. R. T. Burge. Otto H. Kahn. G. L. Smith. Gaetano Merola

Diaghilieff and Selisburg, Pencil Drawing by Pablo Picasso (Museum of Modern Art)

ADOLPH BOLM in *Prince Igor*, 1909

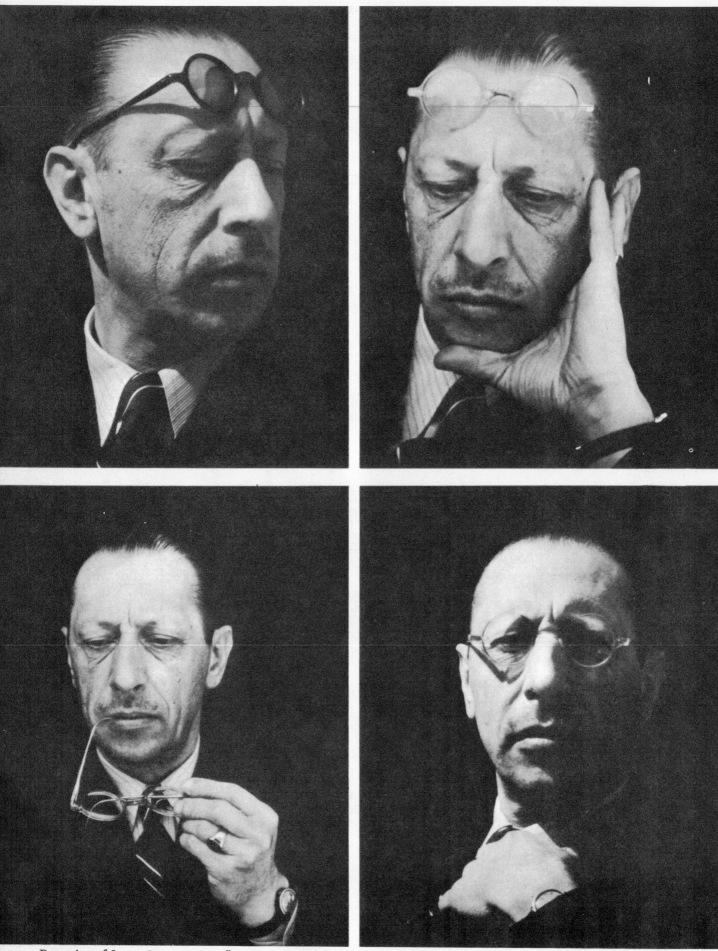

Portraits of IGOR STRAVINSKY (by Edward Weston)

Drawing of STRAVINSKY by Pablo Picasso (Merle Armitage Collection)

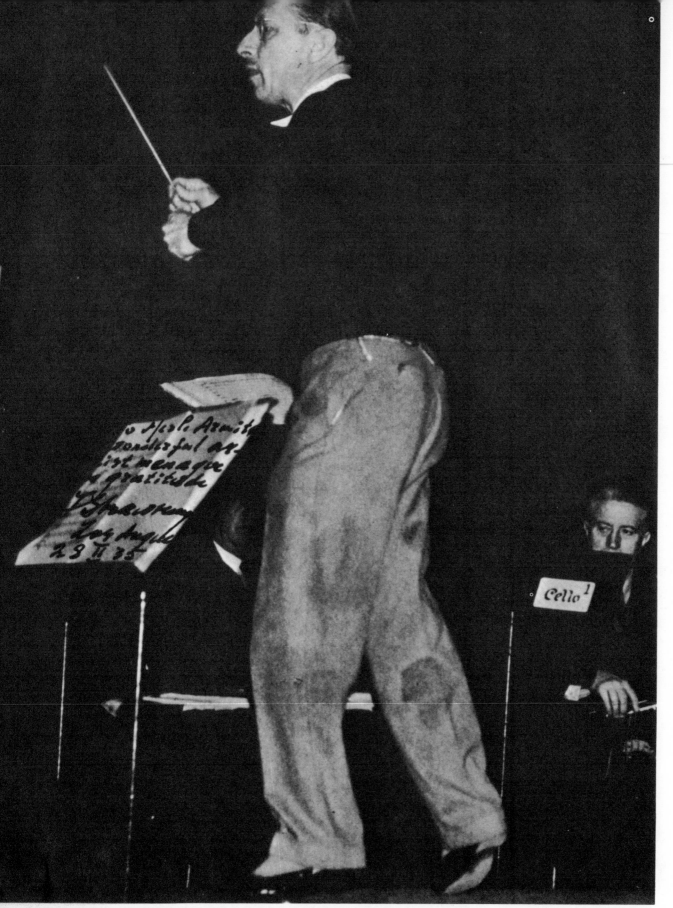

STRAVINSKY Conducting

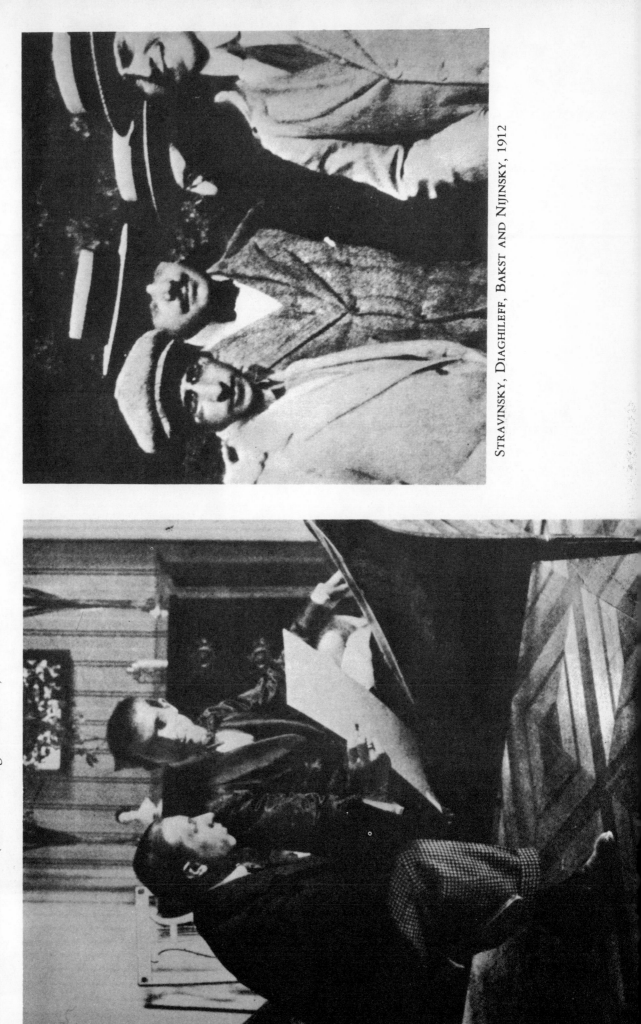

STRAVINSKY AND MASSINE (Merle Armitage Collection)

STRAVINSKY, DIAGHILEFF, BAKST AND NIJINSKY, 1912

Portrait of NIJINSKY (From: The Russian Ballet in Western Europe—Walter Propert)

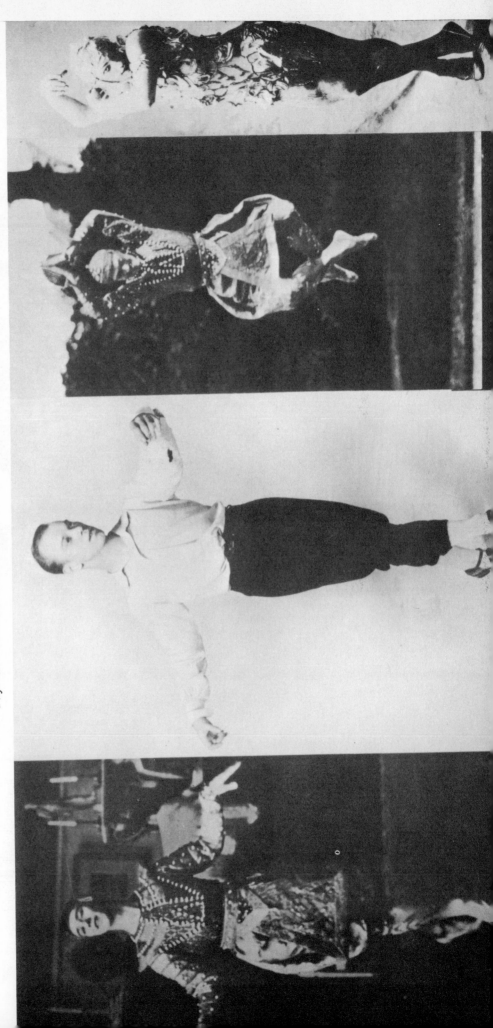

NIJINSKY in Performances and Rehearsal of Le Dieu Bleu (Courtesy: Anatole Chujoy—The Dance News)

NIJINSKY (Merle Armitage Collection)

ANNA PAVLOVA (Merle Armitage Collection)

ANNA PAVLOVA in *The Dying Swan* (Merle Armitage Collection)

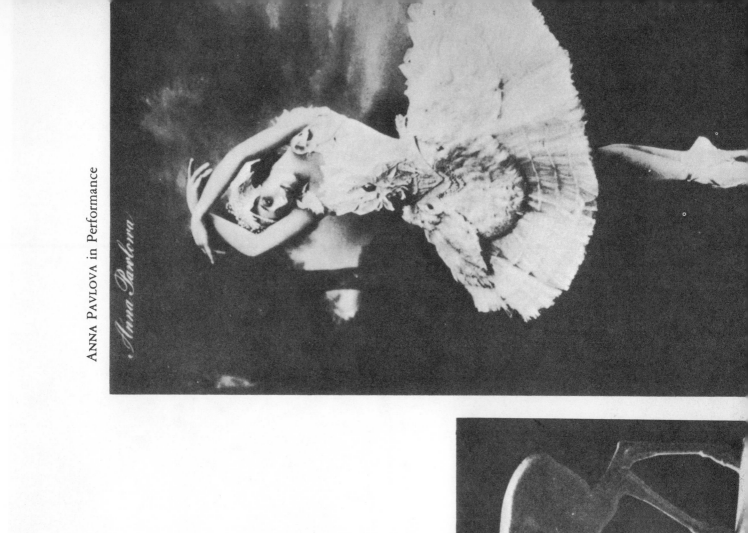

ANNA PAVLOVA in Performance

ANNA PAVLOVA and Deer, Sculpture by Hugo Lederer

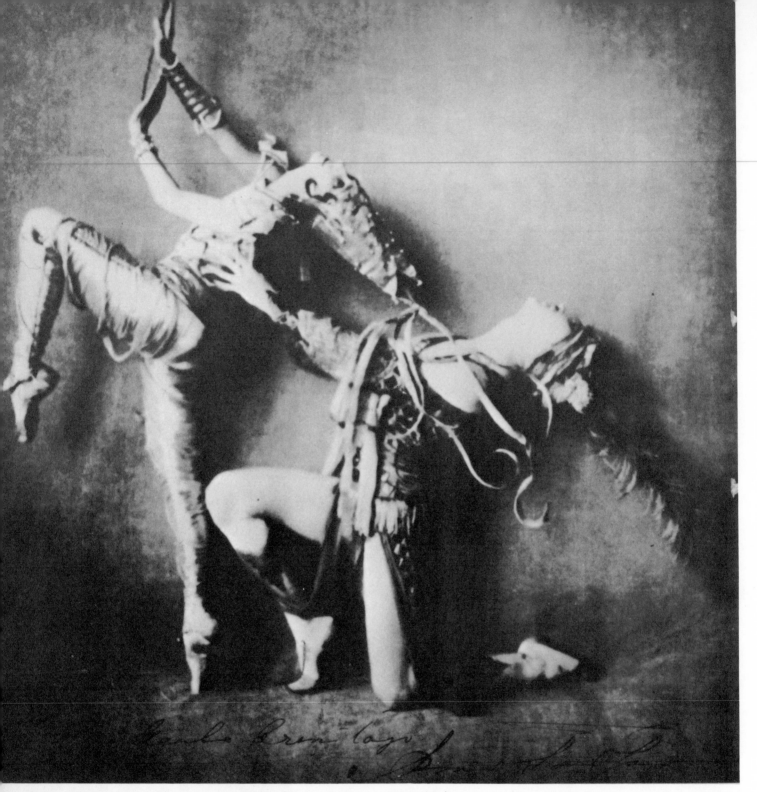

ANNA PAVLOVA AND HERBERT STOWITTS (Merle Armitage Collection)

MIKHAIL MORDKIN (Museum of Modern Art, Dance Archives)

RUTH ST. DENIS as Algerian Dancing Girl, 1920

TED SHAWN in *Credo*

RUTH ST. DENIS AND TED SHAWN

RAMIEL MCGEHEE in Japanese *No* Dance (by Edward Weston) 1918

La Argentina (Catharine A. Bamman Collection)

La Argentina During First American Tour, 1916

Margaret Severn, Exponent of the Benda Masks

RUTH PAGE WITH ADOLPH BOLM BALLET INTIME, 1920

Portrait of LINCOLN KIRSTEIN by Carl Van Vechten

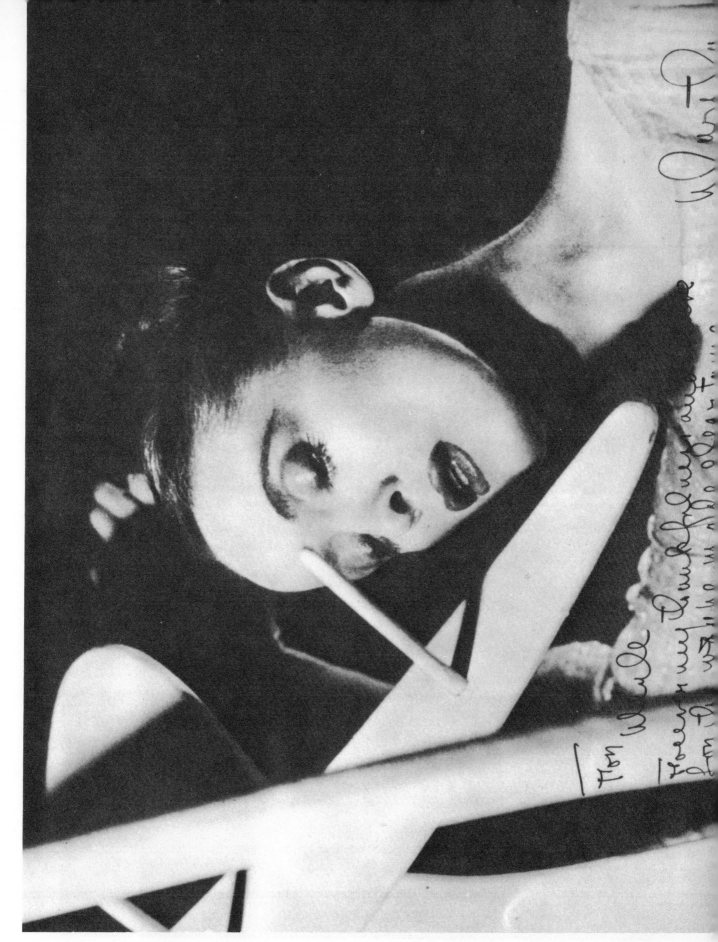

Portrait of MARTHA GRAHAM by Barbara Morgan

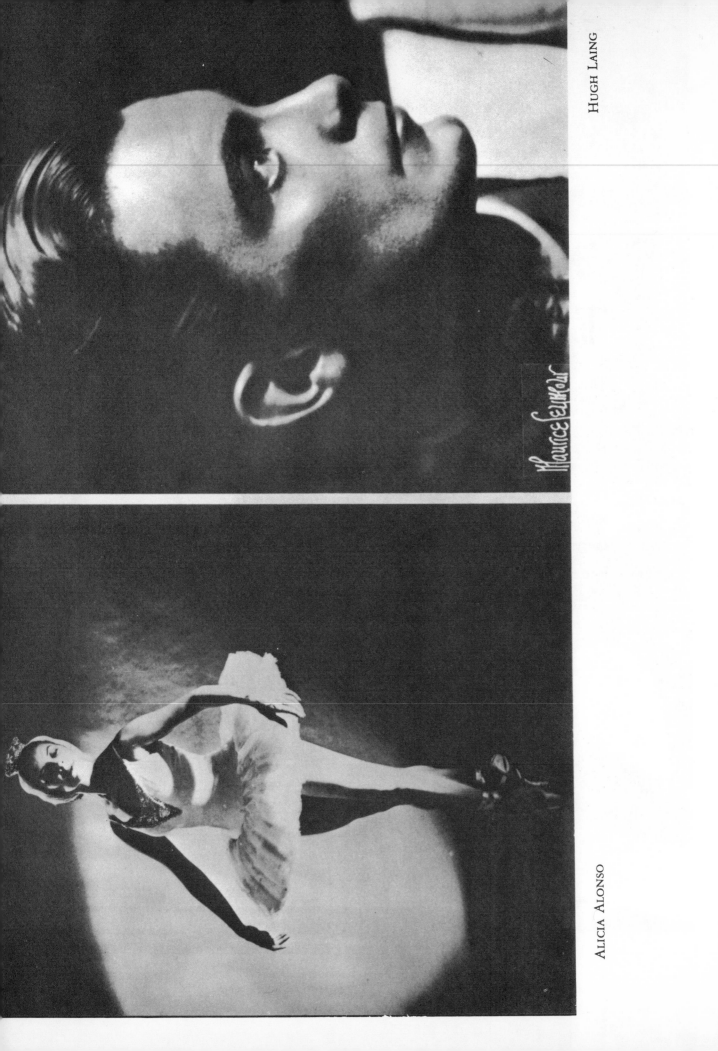

HUGH LAING

ALICIA ALONSO

THE GALLERY

This section includes painting, drawing and sculpture in many periods, relating to the dance. Although there are four groups – *Ancient Art, Abstract Art, Décor and Costumes,* and *Painting, Drawing and Sculpture*–many of the groups overlap and the division is arbitrary. If the reproductions herein give but a hint of the rich world of art which has portrayed the dance, they indicate, nevertheless, how many great artists of every century, country and race, have been caught by the movement of forms in space.

Ancient Art

Algonkian Petroglyph (Smithsonian Institution)

Etruscan Bronze (Arthur Sachs Collection)

Dancing Girls. Tomb of Nenkheptkai, Egypt (From: The Art of Ancient Egypt, Phaidon Press)

Three Dancing Figures. Wall Fragment, Limestone. Egyptian, 2,700 B.C. (Walters Art Gallery, Baltimore)

Female Dancer and Acrobat. Painting on Limestone about 1180 B.C. Egypt (From: The Art of Ancient Egypt, Phaidon Press)

Dancing Girl. Greek, 4th Century B.C. Terra-cotta. (Walters Art Gallery, Baltimore)

Youth and Dancing Girl. Greek. Interior of Kylix. 5th Century

Left: *Reclining Youth*, Etruscan Bronze. Right: *Dancers*, Etruscan Bronze. 560-450 B.C. (Metropolitan Museum)

Large Bone Box. Egypt. Coptic. 5th to 7th Century, A.D. (Walters Art Gallery, Baltimore)

Musicians and One Dancer. Stone Sculpture. Chinese, 8th Century. T'ang Dynasty (Freer Gallery of Art, Washington)

Dancers, from the Etruscan Caves (Merle Armitage Collection)

Greco-Italian Vase (Walters Art Gallery, Baltimore)

Greek Dancer (enlarged detail) Attic (Walters Art Gallery)

Iris, East Pedimant of Parthenon (British Museum, London)

Dancers, Angkor Thom (Photograph by Gerald Coward)

Devata. Angkor Vat (Photograph by Gerald Coward)

Apsaras, Angkor Vat (Photograph by Gerald Coward)

Dancing Apsaras. Cambodia 9th to 12th Century. Bronze (Museum of Fine Arts, Boston)

Bala Krsna. Southern India, 16th Century. Bronze (Albright Art Gallery, Buffalo)

Dancer. India. Bronze (Photograph by Gerald Coward)

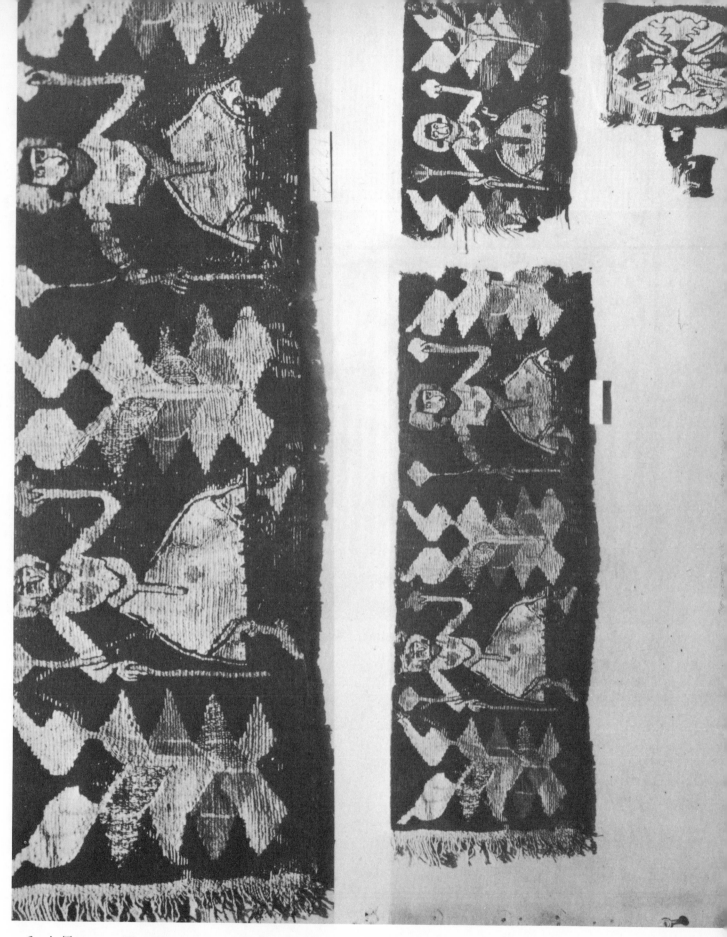

Coptic Tapestry. The Figures are Probably Saints. 6th or 7th Century. (The Textile Museum of the District of Columbia)

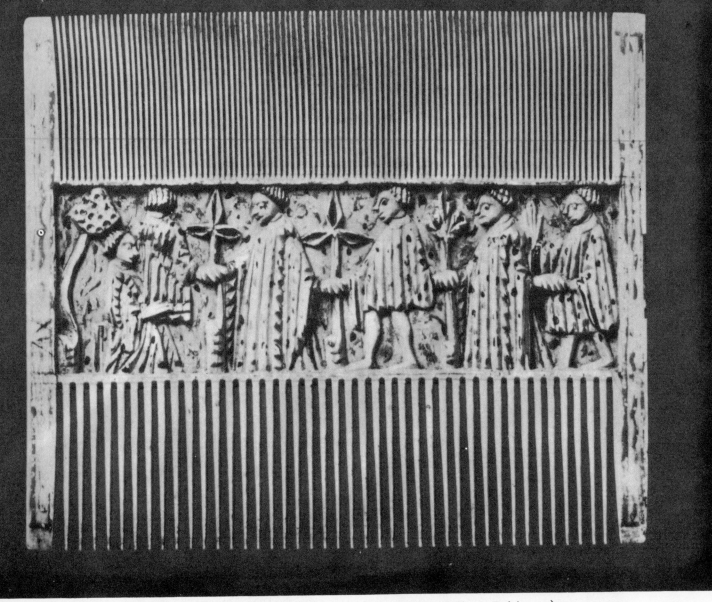

Ivory Comb. Scenes from a Romance. Italian, 15th Century (Walters Art Gallery, Baltimore)

॥प्रियालिनोक्रोमलविमलमनकमलासीसधीसाध
कमलाञ्पोली ह्हायकमलसनालके तरुरकेधुनि
सुनिलोर्कलहंसनिकें चाकिचाकिपरचारुवेडवाम
रालकों । कवनिकेसाडखलारनिमखुचलारलाविकिल
वकिजालकटतटवालके सरंहरंदोलतिविलोकतिदम
निहे मतिहेरंहरंहरेचलतिहरतिमनलालके । पिय्राल
निलं ॥ चपलाघट्मोरकिरीटलसेमधवाघनसालवडा
वतदे हडुगावे श्रावतदेडुवज्ञादमित्रमयूरनबाड
तद्या विदेषितदूतलोचनचानिकि चित्रकोतापतुरु
वतदे घनस्याखुघनोघनबेषधरेजुवबनुतेबज्ञ्या
वतदा ॥ मदहावलच्एणें ॥ घरनघमघतापेगर्बुब्रा
वऊुलावे ॥ तिनकेतरुनिविकारतेंञपजिपरेंमदहाव

Krishna Dancing. Indian Manuscript (Metropolitan Museum of Art)

Chinese Officer Dances for His Lady. Old Chinese Dolls (International Studio)

Nataraja, Lord of the Dance. India, 14th to 15th Century (The Cleveland Museum of Art)

ETRUSCAN DANCER FROM CHIUSI. BRONZE

Abstract Art

The Three Dancers. Pablo Picasso. Painting, 1925 (Museum of Modern Art, New York)

Antikristo by Michael Lekakis

Figure. Jacques Lipchitz. Bronze, 1926-30 (Museum of Modern Art)

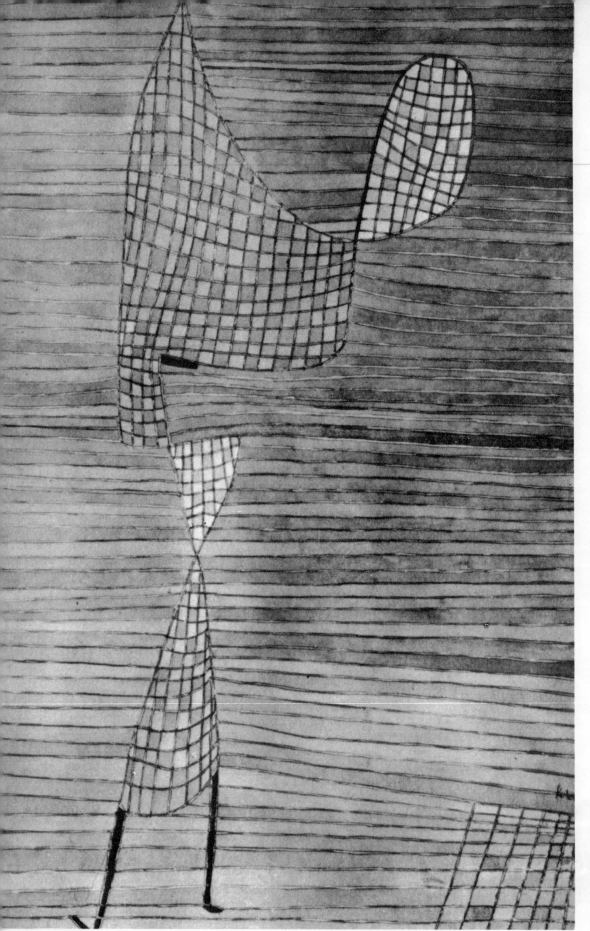

Square Dancer by Paul Klee, 1934 (Collection Marian Willard)

Group de Ballet. Paul Klee, 1923 (Collection of Pierre Loeb)

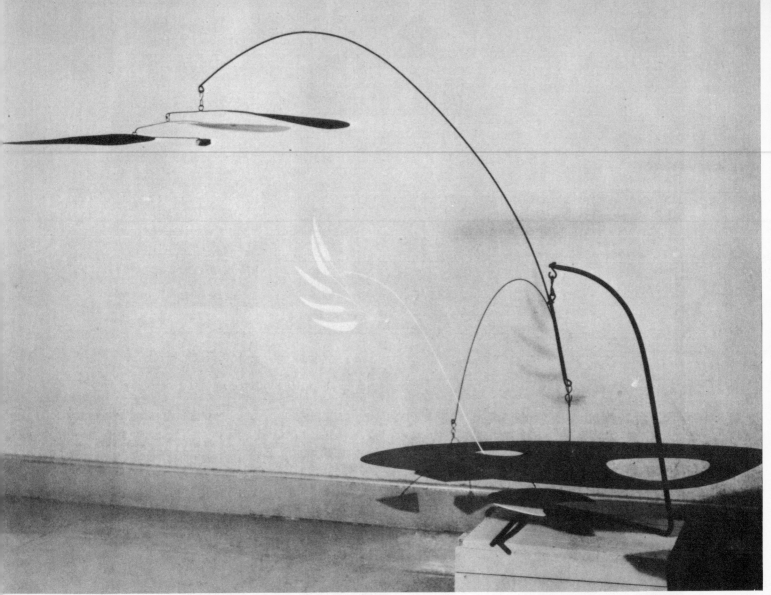

Mobile by Alexander Calder (Kurt Valentin Collection)

Sirtos in Crayon. Michael Lekakis

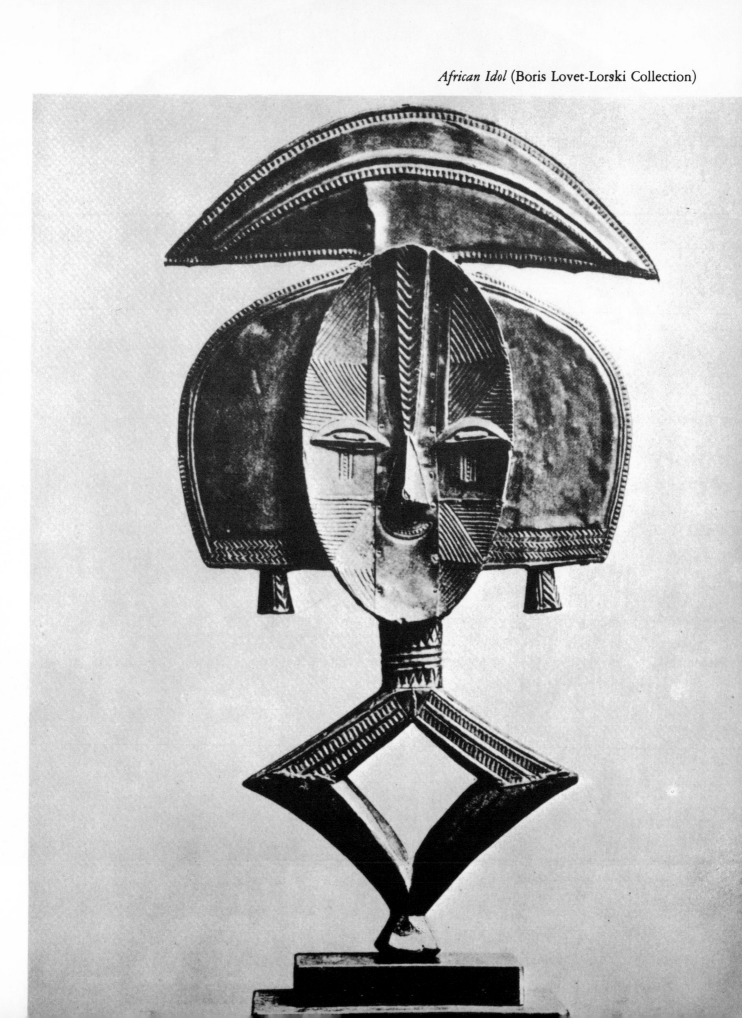

Dance Group by Amedee Ozenfant, 1930 (Passedoit Gallery)

Dancer and Tambourin. Pablo Picasso. Aquetint (Buchholz Gallery)

Dancer by Carlus Dyer. Lithograph (Merle Armitage Collection)

Decor and Costumes

Backdrop for Les Presages, 1933. Andre Masson (Museum of Modern Art)

Sketch for Italian Symphony by Eugene Berman (Museum of Modern Art)

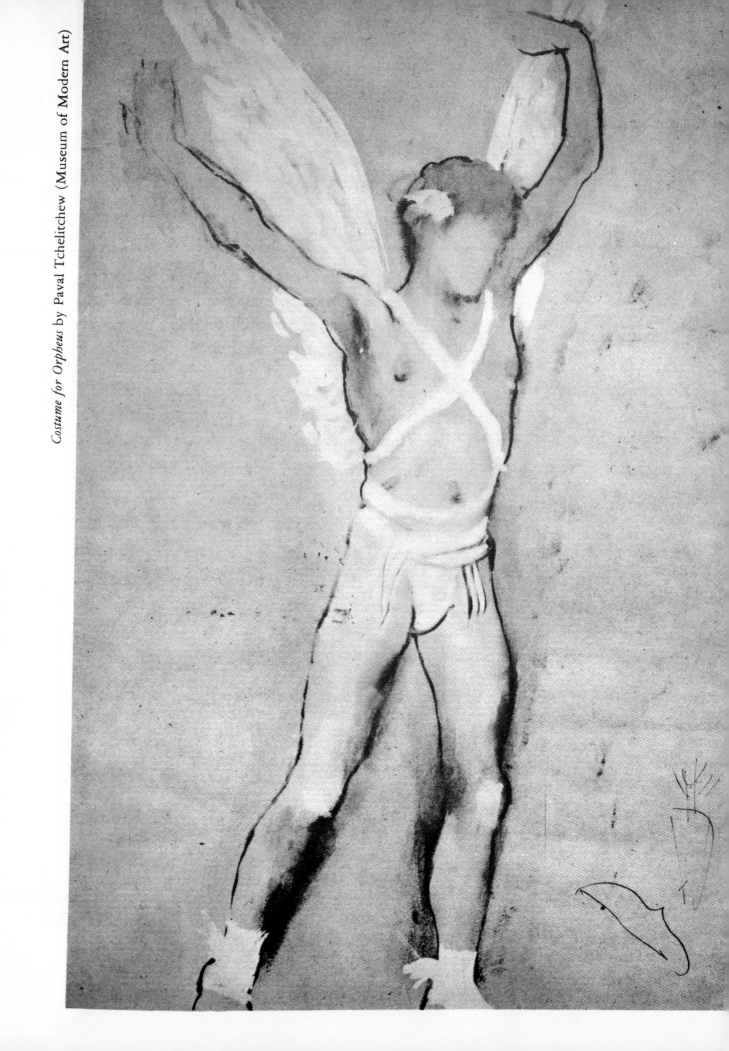

Costume for Orpheus by Paval Tchelitchew (Museum of Modern Art)

Backdrop for Petrouchka by Remisoff (Steinway Collection)

Two Ballet Scenes by Jean de Botton (Dalzell Hatfield Gallery)

Costume for Filling Station by Paul Cadmus, 1938 (Museum of Modern Art)

Costumes for Transcendence by Franklin Watkins (Museum of Modern Art)

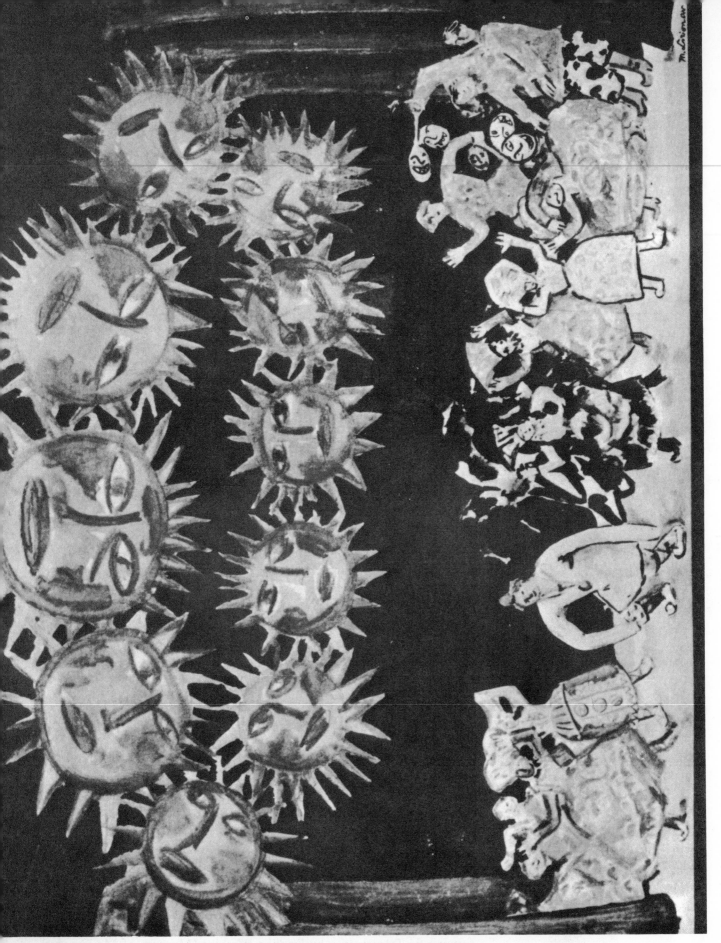

Curtain for Soleil de Nuit by M. Larionov (Russian Ballet in Western Europe)

Curtain for Foire Russe by N. Gontcharova (Russian Ballet in Western Europe)

Sketch for Carnaval Performance. Karsavina, Nijinsky and Bolm

Costume by Picasso (Russian Ballet in Western Europe)

Drawing of Adolph Bolm as the Prince in Thamar by Bakst

Pierrot Costume by Bakst (Courtesy: Fine Art Society, London)

Costume for L'Oiseau de Feu by Bakst (Fine Art Society, London)

Costume for L' Apres midi d'un Faune (Nijinsky) by Bakst (Fine Art Society, London)

Painting, Drawing
and Sculpture

Portrait of Leon Bakst by Modigliani (Decorative Art of Leon Bakst)

The Dancer by Karl Zerbe. Encaustic. 1943 (The Downtown Gallery)

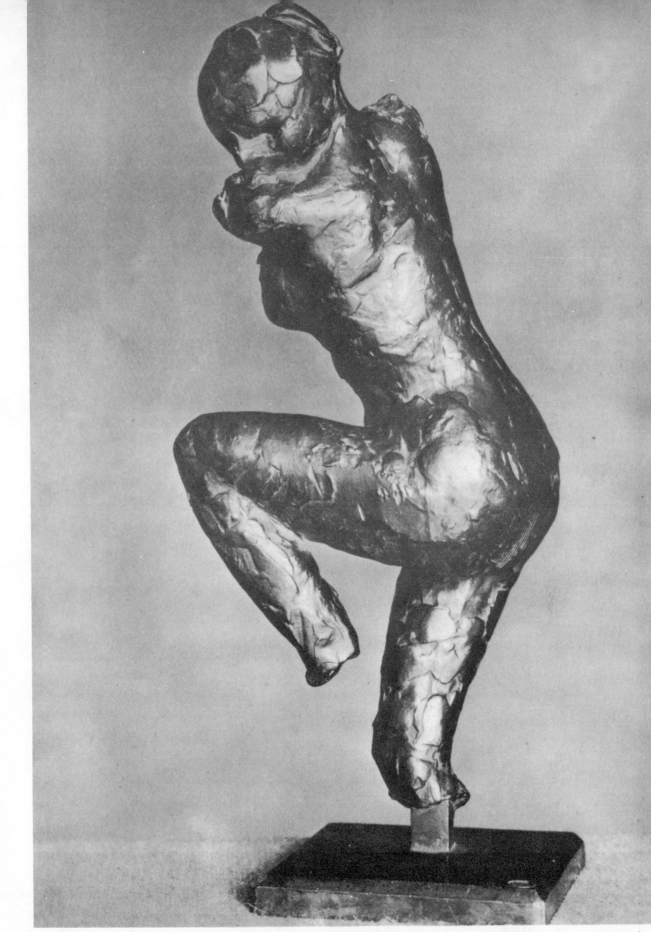

Dancer by Degas. Bronze (Curt Valentin)

Degas

The Foyer by Degas (Metropolitan Museum of Art)

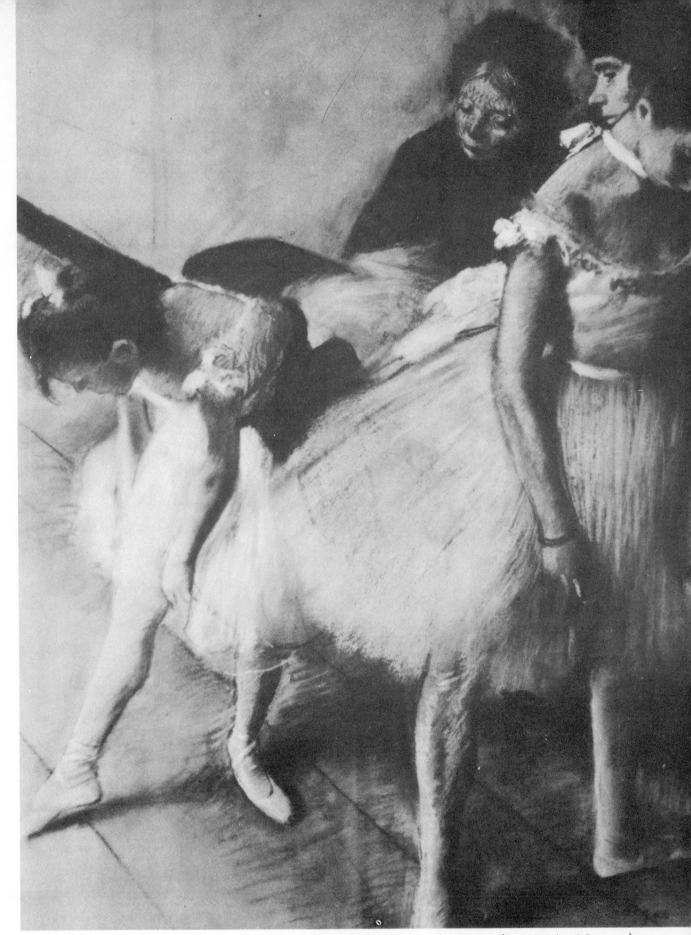

Danseuse a la Toilette by Degas (Denver Art Museum)

Ballet Girls by H. D. Edgar Degas. Pastel (The Cleveland Museum of Art)

Primitive Dancer by Boris Lovet-Lorski

Icaria (Sun Dance) by Boris Lovet-Lorski (Wildenstein and Company)

Tango by Elie Nadelman (Scott and Fowles)

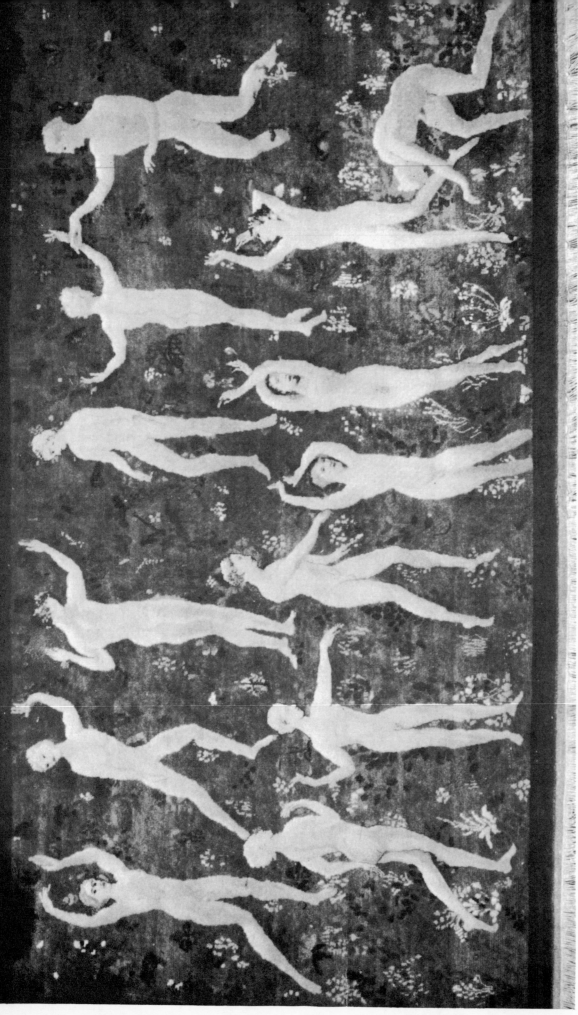

Tapestry by Arthur B. Davies (Mrs. John D. Rockefeller Collection)

Dancer by Elie Nadelman (Dial Magazine)

The Princess in Firebird by Marc Chagall (Museum of Modern Art)

Ballet Dancers by Marc Chagall. Gouache (Pierre Matisse Gallery)

Ballet Dancer by Russell Cowles (Mr. and Mrs. Dalzell Hatfield Collection)

Rate de Ballet by John Carroll (Honolulu Academy of Arts)

Kreutzberg Dancing by Remisoff

Fetish Dancers by George Gershwin (Ira Gershwin)

Japanese Woman Dancer by Kiyonobu (Ledoux Collection)

Actor, Ichikawa Clan by Kiyotada (Ledoux Collection)

Spirit of the Dance by William Zorach (The Downtown Gallery)

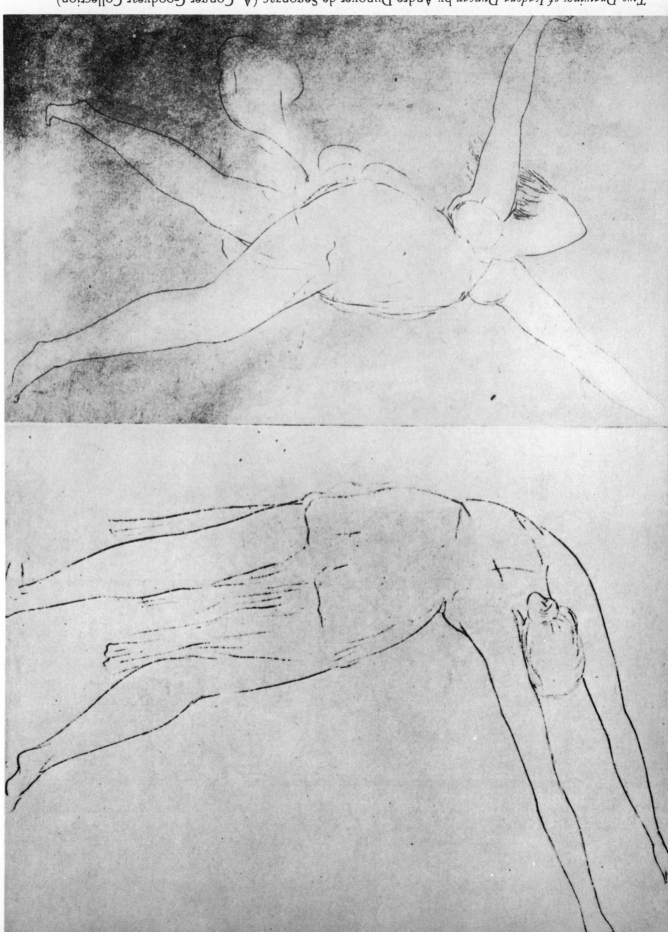

Two Drawings of Isadora Duncan by Andre Dunoyer de Segonzac (A. Conger Goodyear Collection)

Dancer by Henri Matisse (Pierre Matisse Gallery)

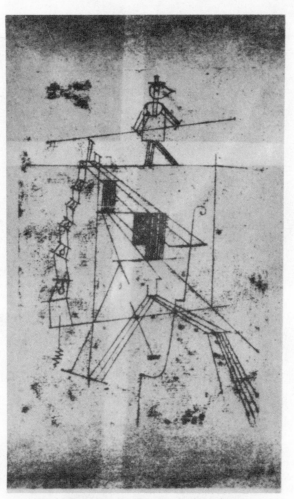

Tight Rope Walker by Paul Klee (Karl
Nierendorf Gallery)

Navajo Feather Dance by Andy Tsihnahjinnie   *Devil Dance* by Allan Hauser (Mrs. Charles H. Dietrich Collection)

Zia Pueblo Dancers by **Ma-Pe-Wi** (Dietrich Collection)

Drawing by Salvador Dali (Dalzell Hatfield Gallery)

Drawing by Salvador Dali (Dalzell Hatfield Gallery)

Primavera by Botticelli

Kongo Voodoo by Allan Clark. Bronze (Dalzell Hatfield Gallery)

Nude by Gaston Lachaise. *Drawing* (Brooklyn Museum)

After Martha Graham's Herodiade, by Charlotte Trowbridge

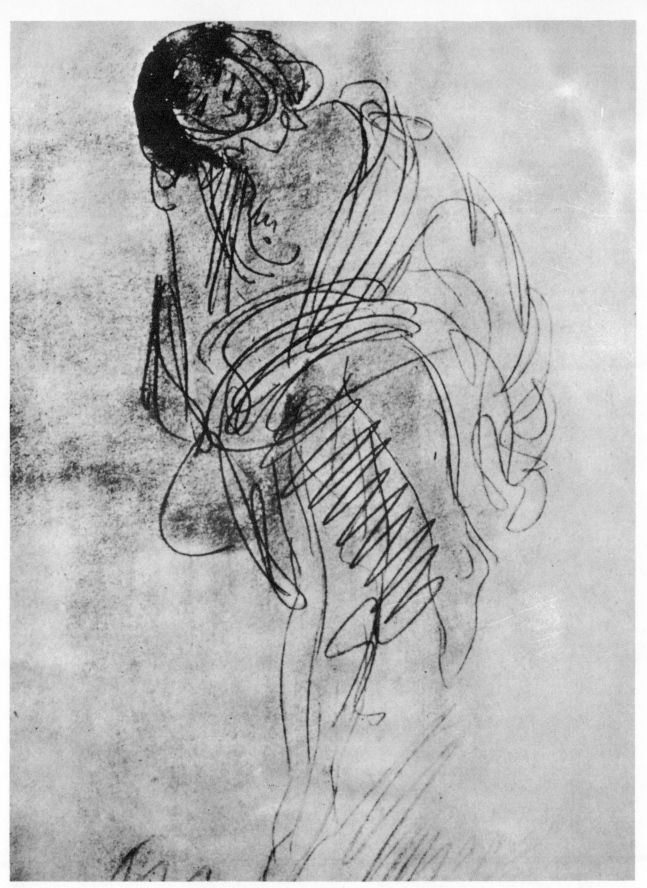

Drawing of Isadora Duncan by Rodin (Musee Rodin and Theatre Arts)

Drawing of Dancer by Auguste Rodin (Carl O. Schniewind Collection)

The Pink Sash by Louis Kronberg (Metropolitan Museum of Art)

The Dancer by Renoir (National Gallery of Art, Washington—Widener Collection)

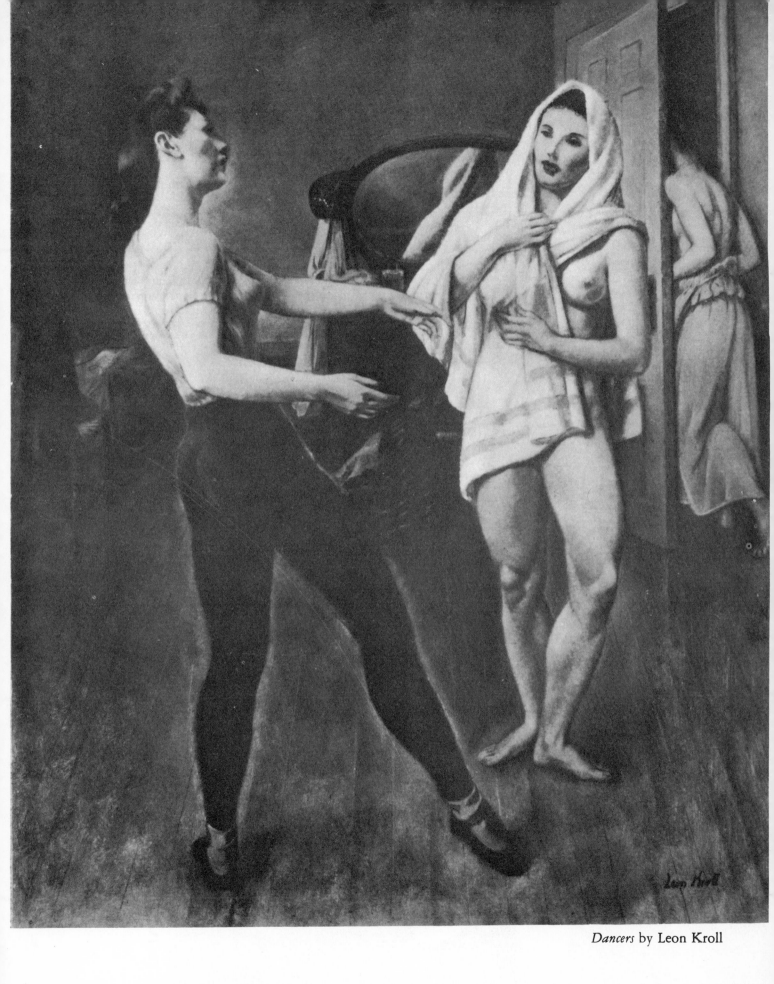

Dancers by Leon Kroll

Dancer by Georg Kolbe (Kurt Wolff Verlag)

Dancer by Maurice Sterne (Los Angeles Museum)

The Dance by Andre Derain (Russian Ballet in Western Europe)

Dancer, by Eric Gill (International Studio)

Portrait of Isadora Duncan by Arthur B. Davies (Ferargil Galleries)

The Dancer by Ignacio Zuloaga (Merle Armitage Collection)

Intermission by Moses Soyer (A.C.A. Gallery)

Dancing at the Savoy by Jacob Lawrence (The Downtown Gallery)

Four Drawings of Isadora Duncan by Bourdelle (Libraire de France and Theatre Arts)

The Dance. Bernhard Hoetger (Maier-Krieg Collection)

Mia Slavenska Dancing by Etienne Ret

Portrait of Massine by Picasso (Russian Ballet in Western Europe)

Afternoon of a Faun by Dan Lutz (Dalzell Hatfield Galleries)

BALLET NOMENCLATURE

Through the centuries there has envolved a nomenclature which has become an international ballet language. Some of the more fundamental terms in the vocabulary of the ballet dancer and the cognoscenti are listed as a guide for the growing ballet audience. These have been selected and compiled, with comments, by a ballet authority, Ann Barzell, and are used with her permission:

adagio – slow movements. When performed by one dancer an adagio involves taking various positions while balancing on one leg. A dance for a man and woman is often called an adagio; the man's chief function is to support his partner as she takes various poses and pirouettes.

aplomb – balance, the dancer's ability to hold a position or pose.

arabesque – position of a dancer wherein the leg is raised in back, the opposite arm usually stretched forward. There are many types of arabesque depending on the position of the body and arms.

attitude – a position wherein one leg is raised in the back, well bent at the knee. There is also a front attitude.

balletomane – an enthusiastic ballet "fan." The balletomane will see any ballet hundreds of times and still come to see it again.

batterie – steps whose execution includes the beating together of the calves of the legs.

bourrée – quick steps on both toes which make the dancer seem to float across the stage.

choreographer – the individual who invents and arranges the sequence of steps and dances in a ballet.

choreography – the sequence of steps and dances in a ballet.

coda – the last part of a classical pas de deux.

développé – unfolding the leg in any direction. The flowing quality with which this is accomplished is an index to the dancer's style.

divertissement – one or more solo or group dances either interpolated in a ballet as an entertainment or presented as a suite of dances.

elevation – the ability to jump high.

enchainement – a combination of steps that constitute a dance phrase.

entrechat – a jump from fifth position wherein the feet are crossed in mid-air and the calves of the legs beaten together before landing again in fifth position.

fouetté – a step done with a whipping movement. A fouetté pirouette is a turn performed on one leg while the other whips in and out at each revolution.

jeté – a leap. The big leap with which the male dancer often makes an entrance or exit is a *grand jeté*.

pas – literally a step. It is also used to designate a dance as pas seul (solo), pas de trois (dance for three), etc.

pas de deux – dance for two. The grand pas de deux of the ballerina and her partner is designed to exhibit virtuosity and consists of an adagio for both dancers followed by solo variations by each and finishing with the coda in which the two dance together.

pirouette – a turn. There are many different kinds of pirouettes depending on the pose assumed, the movement required, the direction taken, etc. The dancer maintains balance by keeping his eyes as long as possible on one spot and seeking it out after each revolution. This is called spotting and makes the dancer's head seem to be snapping from side to side.

plié – the bending of the knees. All jumps and relevés take off and finish in demi-plié. Heel must be lowered to maintain balance. The ease of the demi-plié has a great deal to do with the quality of a dancer's movement.

pointes – the tips of the toes in toe dancing. Though invented to achieve the unearthly aspect required in 19th Century ballets, pointe work today is more an aid to the clean line that is modern design and the excitement that is theatre.

port de bras – movement of arms. Good arms are those that move calmly and are well-placed – elbows do not sag, wrists do not droop, there is a clean rounded line – unless choreographic requirements are otherwise.

positions – There are five positions of the feet in ballet dancing. They all require that the legs be turned out from the hips down:

> *1st position:* heels together, toes out
>
> *2nd position:* same as first, but feet 12 inches apart
>
> *3rd position:* heel of one foot at the instep of the other
>
> *4th position:* one foot placed about 12 inches in front of the other
>
> *5th position:* heel of one foot placed at toe of other

regisseur – the individual in charge of presentations and of rehearsals. This requires a knowledge of all the roles in all the ballets.

terre-à-terre – steps that do not require jumping.

tutu – the many skirted tarletan or net costume worn by dancers.

ACKNOWLEDGMENTS

Indebtedness is acknowledged to the individuals, institutions and firms who have rendered invaluable service to this project, including:

Individuals

George Amberg, Elsa Armitage, Ann Barzell, Donald J. Bear, Adolph Bolm, Gladys Caldwell, Anatole Chujoy, Jean Corle, E. E. Cummings, Salvador Dali, Mrs. Charles H. Dietrich, Carlos Dyer, Mrs. Emil Ganso, Rosamond Gilder, Ruth Goode, A. Conger Goodyear, Edith Halpert, Ruth and Dalzell Hatfield, Erick Hawkins, Louis Horst, Jean Kellogg, Lincoln Kirstein, Louis V. Ledoux, Pierre Matisse, Barbara Morgan, P. G. Napolitano, Karl Nierendorf, Frederick Newlin Price, Walter Propert, Daniel Catton Rich, Carl O. Schniewind, James Johnson Sweeney, Charlotte Trowbridge, Curt Valentin, Edward Weston, Ernest Weyhe, Marian Willard, Kurt Wolff, and L. E. Behymer.

Photographers

Marcus Blechman, Bouchard, Lansing Brown, Gerald Coward, Louise Dahl-Wolf, Arnold Eagle, Arnold Genthe, Maurice Goldberg, Paul Hansen, Victor Jessen, Ernest Knee, George Platt Lynes, Mishkin, Gjon Mili, Barbara Morgan, Gerda Peterich, Maurice Seymour, Soichi Sunami, Carl Van Vechten, Brett Weston, and Edward Weston.

Firms

A. C. A. Gallery, New York; John Lane, The Bodley Head Limited, London; The Buchholz Gallery, New York; The Dance News, New York; The Dial Magazine, New York; The Downtown Gallery, New York; The Ferargil Gallery, New York; The Fine Art Society, Limited, London; Dalzell Hatfield Gallery, Los Angeles and New York; Hurok Attractions Inc., New York; Passedoit Gallery, New York; Frank K. M. Rehn, Inc., New York; Steinway and Sons, New York; Theatre Arts, New York; E. Weyhe Gallery, New York; The Willard Gallery, New York; and Houghton Mifflin Company, Boston.

Institutions

The Albright Art Gallery, Buffalo; The Art Institute, Chicago; The Cleveland Museum of Art; The Denver Art Museum; Freer Gallery of Art, Washington; Laboratory of Anthropology, Sante Fe; The Library of Congress, Washington; The Los Angeles Museum; The Los Angeles Public Library; The Metropolitan Museum of Art, New York; Museum of Fine Arts, Boston; The Museum of Modern Art, New York; Museum of Navajo Ceremonial Art, Santa Fe; National Gallery of Art, Washington; The New York Public Library; Santa Barbara Museum of Art; Textile Museum of the District of Columbia; Walters Art Gallery, Baltimore; and The Brooklyn Museum.

INDEX